ONE FOLD, ONE SHEPHERD

ONE FOLD, ONE SHEPHERD

The challenge to the post-Reformation Church

George Bennet

GEOFFREY
CHAPMAN

Geoffrey Chapman
A Cassell imprint
Wellington House, 125 Strand, London WC2R 0BB
215 Park Avenue South, New York, NY 10003

First published 1996

British Library Cataloguing-in-Publication Data
A catalogue record for this book is available from the British Library.

ISBN 0-225-66821-1

Cover picture: based on a wall mosaic (c. AD 530)
in the apse of the church of San Vitale, Ravenna.

Designed and typeset by Kenneth Burnley at Irby, Wirral, Cheshire.
Printed and bound in Great Britain by
Biddles Ltd, of Guildford and King's Lynn

CONTENTS

FOREWORD

This is a most unusual book, in many ways a unique one. It is also a very uncomfortable book. It will disturb the settled convictions of almost everyone who reads it – I know it disturbed mine. But all this is just a different way of saying it is a powerful book, which presses its case remorselessly and with charity, but above all with clarity. If it is not an easy book to live with, it is not a hard book to read.

George Bennet was an Anglican vicar with opinions on the protestant side of the Church of England (nowadays called evangelical). Coming from Puritan East Anglia, he may even be regarded as a spiritual heir of Cromwell's Ironsides. By a difficult mental and spiritual route only he can fully describe, he came at last to a remarkable conclusion. It was not that his protestant convictions were wholly wrong and ought to be abandoned. Others have thought that before. It was that while still holding on to his protestant convictions *he was in the wrong Church.*

Again, others have thought that before. It is not all that uncommon for Anglicans to become Baptists, or Baptists Presbyterians; each searching for a place in which they can be better protestants. But the place George Bennet has selected as the place where he can be a better protestant is *the Church of Rome.* And the Roman Catholic Church is supposed to be the very antithesis of Protestantism.

His close inspection of it convinced him that an astonishing change had taken place in the Catholic Church over the last generation or two, to such an extent that it had incorporated into itself (perhaps four centuries later than it should have done) all the most salient and spirit-filled features of the Protestant Reformation. This is almost like saying – though George is far too humble to frame the thought – that it is not so much he who has joined the Roman Catholic Church as the Roman Catholic Church that has joined him!

This means, for all those Anglicans and Catholics who have struggled with, repented of, yet still cannot see how to resolve their long historical separation, that the time has come to look not so much into each other as into themselves. Catholics have to find the protestant within, this time not as heretic or enemy but as their biblical conscience. Protestants have to rediscover the Catholicizing dynamic that is implicit in their own faith (including a rediscovery of the meaning of a thousand years of church history that has been airbrushed out of their history books).

It does not necessarily mean that protestants all have to follow George Bennet. Maybe none will: who can say? He is a lone pioneer, and probably must remain that way. That is not the point. What he is pleading for is not individual conversion as a solution to church disunity, but corporate convergence as the two branches of the Christian family come to realize that what once divided them need no longer do so. Only one who has stood on both sides of the divide can say this with the sort of understanding George Bennet here supplies. And that is why this book deserves an enduring place in the literature of contemporary Christianity.

CLIFFORD LONGLEY

ACKNOWLEDGEMENTS

Scripture quotations are from the Holy Bible, New International Version, © 1973, 1978, 1984 the International Bible Society. Scripture references are indexed on p. 147.

Quotations from the *Catechism of the Catholic Church* (© 1994 Geoffrey Chapman–Libreria Editrice Vaticana) are indicated by the letters CCC followed by the paragraph number(s): e.g. (CCC 1294). The paragraphs quoted are listed on p. 147.

The quotations on pp. 36, 37 and 38 from the letters of Clement of Rome and Ignatius of Antioch are from the translation by Maxwell Staniforth, *Early Christian Writings*, in the Penguin Classics series. © 1968 Penguin Books Limited.

The quotations from the Fathers on the opening page of each section are from The Office of Readings of The Divine Office, the Liturgy of the Hours according to the Roman Rite, where they will be found as follows:

p. 7 (Pope St Gregory the Great), vol. II, p. 165*
p. 28 (St Augustine), vol. III, p. 580
p. 57 (Pope St Leo the Great), vol. II, p. 357*
p. 77 (St Bernard), vol. III, p. 368*
p. 98 (St Cyril of Jerusalem), vol. III, p. 726

Reproduced by permission of HarperCollins Religious, London.

The quotation on p. 128 from the encyclical *Ad Petri Cathedram* of Pope John XXIII is from the English edition of Vatican Polyglot Press. Reproduced by permission of the Catholic Truth Society, London.

INTRODUCTION

Last year I became a Roman Catholic; before that for 25 years I was a priest in the Church of England. What makes my case different from many others is that my roots in the Church of England are *evangelical*. It is as an *evangelical protestant* that I enter the Catholic Church, and as an evangelical protestant that I accept its teaching and authority.

My protestant friends will blink at such a statement, but I hope to show them how scriptural this position is. Evangelical protestants are not necessarily against the Catholic Church, only against unscriptural teaching. The Reformers of the sixteenth century would never have split the Church if they could have achieved reform any other way. The Reformation which started then has taken a long time to spread all through the Church, but the process is over and has done its work – even in the Catholic Church. If the Catholic Church had been in the sixteenth century what it is now, there would have been no real reason to separate. So why stay apart now?

The Reformation has taken 450 years – at an accelerating pace this century; in the last 30 years since the Second Vatican Council the Catholic Church has changed out of all recognition. In many ways it is now more 'reformed' than most protestant groups. Its modern doctrine of the Church has excellent scriptural arguments to support it, though most catholics are not used to that way of looking at it. An ex-protestant is, I think, in a good position to set out these arguments – and that is one of my purposes in writing this book.

Dr David Edwards, in his recent book *What is Catholicism?* (Mowbray), examines critically the present official teaching of the Catholic Church (mostly as expressed in its newly published Catechism and in its Code of Canon Law of 1983). As we would expect, his treatment is scholarly and well researched; and, as a catholic, I found it enormously generous. But he writes from the *outside*; and I have to say that it is not how I have found the Church in my short experience on the *inside*.

Early last year I joined a group of ex-Anglican priests preparing for reception into the Catholic Church. We were provided with a wide-ranging course by a group of catholic priests and academics. For me the most unexpected part of this experience was hearing the protestant teaching on which I was brought up coming from the lips of these catholics. They were talking of the Church as the people of God, and using biblical models to describe it: the Body of Christ, the Lord's Sheepfold, the Temple of the Holy Spirit, and so on. We heard nothing of the old-fashioned model which saw the Pope at the apex of a pyramid, from whom grace trickled down through bishops and priests to the poor benighted laity at the bottom! The model now was based on the people, whom the hierarchy of the Church was called to serve. Priesthood was seen as bestowed by Christ on the *whole* people of God, but focused in the clergy so that they might serve the needs of God's people through teaching and sacrament. The call to holiness was for all, and not just for an elite few. The vocation to serve Christ in a secular job or in the married state was seen as no less important than the call to celibacy and a separated lifestyle. In no way were the laity to regard themselves as second-class Christians, for they *were* the Church. Continual renewal was looked for at every level of church life; and the task of the clergy was to feed, encourage and enable this. To me this all sounded gloriously familiar, but of course it was without the *innate independence* characteristic of all forms of protestantism.

Catholics know they must reject this spirit of independence that so easily destroys the unity of the Church. Nonetheless they are now detached enough to see God's providential hand behind the sixteenth-century Reformation. The destructions, the burnings, and the appalling injustices (on both sides) were human actions; but all the time God was at work seeking to equip his Church for the task it would have to undertake in the modern world.

The positive thing about the sixteenth-century protestant movement was the new respect for the Bible it generated. Protestants actually started *using* the Bible and finding there the strength that it gives. Many catholics have now learnt to do the same, and it is a joy to see this element of protestantism being rediscovered by them. I say *rediscovered* because it is an ancient part of the catholic tradition and heritage. It can do nothing but good for the special scriptural insights of protestants to be opened up further for catholics; an ex-protestant is, I think, well placed to do that – and here is another purpose I have in writing this book.

A well-defined Faith

Like all evangelicals I always took my stand on the Bible as the authority on which Christian faith should be based. Like anyone with an open mind I have come over the years to value also the full range of the Church's spirituality, including its anglo-catholic forms. I have discovered in the Church of England styles of worship and prayer that others have treasured and preserved; and I can now share in these happily and with conviction. But I remain an evangelical. I suppose I should call myself a *catholic* evangelical – or should it now be an *evangelical* catholic?

To some this will sound like the fuzzy middle ground, where all issues are blurred. But throughout my ministry I have never wanted to compromise on anything truly evangelical or truly catholic. Many evangelicals have vague ideas about the Church and its sacraments; and many catholics seem to have mislaid the authority of Scripture. I always wanted to be clear and definite in both areas. It is only by being definite that we can eliminate the vagueness in much modern Christian thinking. A catholic who was once a protestant should be well equipped to do that; this too is my aim in this book.

This definiteness does not, in my view, exclude liberal thinking in the Church. Christian teaching must always be based on good scholarship; and progress comes only through genuine intellectual exploration. I was trained as a scientist, and for twenty years before ordination I taught physics and wrote books about it. I have plenty of room for liberals; and there is scope enough in our situation for new thinking, and particularly for a scientific insight.

A universal Church

English protestants tend to think of the Catholic Church as a rather un-English institution. When they attend a catholic Mass they express surprise at how like their own service it seems. But why *surprise*? The catholics in England are as English as the rest of us, and just as much a part of the English cultural scene.

The feeling that catholicism is foreign needs to be faced, for it exposes a real tension, always there in the Church, between the local and the universal. The Church must be local if it is to mean anything in our lives; and to be local it must be not only English, but essentially at home in this town or that village. But at the same time the Church is universal, with a mission to the whole world. This is the perspective that the post-Reformation Church needs to regain, and we must resist the temptation to retreat into small-island parochialism. The word 'catholic' means 'universal'; and this is the special gift of the Catholic Church to the rest of us. The Church of England too has spread over most of the world; but like all the separated Churches, the more it spreads, the more it tends to fragment along national lines.

For all its faults, the Church of England has been a potent force for good among our people. I was brought up and educated in the mainstream of the Church of England. I received from it my formation as a Christian, and am profoundly grateful for the rich spiritual heritage it bequeathed me. Its comprehensiveness has made room within it, or near it, for a wealth of varying spiritual traditions, sometimes too many for comfort! The richest aspect of my ministry has been the partnership I have enjoyed down the years with so many fine Christians, lay and clerical, and not only Anglican.

But this same comprehensiveness makes it a Church very difficult to hold together, even at the local level. Nationally, it is full of compromises and accommodations. It is too English to be universal. There is no way a worldwide Church can work like that. We need a new vision of the universality of the Church of Christ and of its role in the world. As a new catholic I have a fresh vision of this, and I hope in this book to be able to share it with others.

A missionary Church

The Church has always seen itself as a missionary organization; and Christians in England now recognize our most important mission field as the one on our own doorstep, among our own people, few of whom now have any significant contact with the Church in any form. There is still a certain wealth of folk memory from our Christian past, and alongside it a fairly general respect for the person of Jesus Christ; but little else. And we have the difficult task of learning once more to communicate our faith to the English people.

However, we are not working in virgin soil, for English history has deep Christian roots. For over 1,300 years our culture and language have developed in a Christian setting. Our national life has drawn from many sources, but always (until recently) the nation has sheltered under a Christian umbrella that held it all together. Our people may have little Christian experience, but they cannot be treated as altogether pagan, for the language and thought-forms for talking to them of Christ are all there waiting to be used.

This poses a problem for the Catholic Church in England. At one time it cultivated its own particular jargon, for it needed to distance itself somewhat from protestant ways and present itself as more than just English. But wherever the Church goes it must always learn to use the language and culture of the local people. In England it confronts a culture with a well-formed religious language of its own, which has developed almost entirely within protestantism. This is the language catholics must use if they want to evangelize the English people. The Catholic Church finds this transition fairly difficult, though it is amazing how far it has come just in one generation. Catholic hymn books are now full of protestant items, as well as the songs and choruses of our own generation (mostly from protestant sources); and all the Bible translations familiar to protestants are now in common use among catholics.

But they have still to accept that there is a need in modern England for catholic apologetics. It is not enough just to say 'This is what the Church teaches'. Those not in the catholic fold deserve to be shown how reasonable and coherent catholic doctrine is, and how well it belongs in the world we know. This should be done in our own religious language – which is the language of protestantism. A major part of my purpose in writing this book has been to help catholics see how this may be done.

Running the Church

All protestant Churches have a problem with Church government. They claim to follow Scripture; but there has to be some way of taking the practical decisions, and of settling, amongst other things, what is *scriptural*. In sixteenth-century Europe several kings were powerful enough to dictate how the Vatican should control the Church in their countries. But in England the authority of the Pope came to be denied completely, and the king in parliament became the established decision-making body for all purposes, including the doctrinal regulation of the Church. This gave the Church of England an inbuilt instability that was far from healthy. At first each new monarch brought his or her own redefinition of the Church and its doctrine – Henry, Edward, Mary, Elizabeth, James – each made their changes, sometimes drastically. Only after regicide, bloody civil war, and revolution, did the Church of England come to be embodied in a constitutional settlement that seemed permanent and stable.

However, even constitutions change and adapt; and now, 300 years on, a parliament that was meant to be the stable anchor of the Church finds itself rather embarrassed at having to consider legislation for a body to which only a minority of its members belong. In practice the General Synod now takes the decisions; and the question that haunts the Church is: Who regulates doctrinal development? The parliamentary model suggests that the General Synod is completely free in the matter, but few Christians are entirely happy with that. Until recently we assumed an unwritten rule that nothing would be done to undermine the received faith and order of the Church. But there is no agreement on the content of that faith and order. Evangelicals insist that nothing be enacted contrary to Scripture; but no one can force the General Synod to adopt that rule – or stick to it, if it does. Besides, can even evangelicals agree on what is allowed by Scripture?

The modern Church of England is a kind of federation of different Christian outlooks – catholic, evangelical, liberal, etc. No one party has ever quite gained the upper hand. It has led sometimes to bitter battles of words – or worse! Mostly the Church has lived with the tension, and has used it to hold before the English people the different strands of the ancient faith we have received. But it has never been a united Church with a clear identity and purpose, other than in being English. Now in the post-Reformation situation it is time for protestants to consider again how Church government should be managed. It is not as though the Lord had nothing to say on the subject. Are they quite sure that the papal model is mistaken? Our predecessors in the sixteenth century did not at first think so. An ex-protestant who has recently wrestled with this problem may have helpful thoughts to offer. Later in this book I offer them.

The best theology is always simple – like the teaching of our Lord – and speaks easily to our consciences, whatever party label it seems to carry; and I am aiming for that sort of simplicity. I want to get beyond the negative arguments that have troubled us in the past. I have noticed that in Christian dialogue people are usually right in what they affirm, and wrong in what they deny. For what we affirm is our experience of God, and that is real to us and life-giving. The things we deny are those we do not understand – and there we do well to keep our mouths shut! My purpose is to engage in some provocative lateral thinking based on the great universal affirmations of Christendom, and so find new perspectives to make old problems look different. I want to free the log-jam in Christian thinking, so that we can move forward in the Lord's purposes towards a universal Church.

George Bennet
Wymondham, Norfolk, 1995

A CHURCH
ON THE FRINGE
The challenge of history

Through his love we seek in Britain brothers whom we do not know, and by his gift we find those whom in our ignorance we were seeking. For who could fully tell the joy that has sprung up in the hearts of all the faithful because the race of the Angles, through the grace of Almighty God and the labours of your brotherhood, has had the light of holy faith poured out on it and the darkness of error driven away?

Pope St Gregory the Great, sixth century, *Letters*, Book 9, 36

1: A SYNOD THAT FAILED

In October 663 there met in the coastal town of Streonaeshalch a Synod of the English Church. The place later came to be known as Whitby. Abbess Hilda and her nuns from the local convent ably hosted the Synod, and all the top people were there. It was one of those familiar Church occasions when a vociferous minority has to be heard; but the real objective is to tweak them into line with everyone else.

The result was therefore a foregone conclusion. Certainly the lay chairman, King Oswy, arrived with his mind made up, and saw it as his job to steer the Synod with good humour and a light touch towards the inevitable final decision. Unity was apparently restored. The dissidents could withdraw with dignity to remote monasteries where they would do no harm, and the Church returned to the task of taking the Gospel to the English people.

The Synod of Whitby, however, settled nothing. It found a way of moving forward – often the only thing the Church can do in the face of strong disagreements. But the deep-down issues remained unresolved, and still are, thirteen centuries later.

An isolated Church
The trouble came from the long isolation of the Celtic Church in the dark ages. Driven into remote Irish monasteries by waves of pagan marauders, it developed its own patterns of church life. It was not that

they tried to be different; but they had to adapt to survive. More than two centuries passed before effective contact with Rome was resumed, quite enough for the Church in Ireland and the British churches spawned from it to develop their own very Celtic flavour.

The Irish monasteries were literally fortresses – they had to be. The control and protection of the community was in the hands of the abbot. The monastery was a base for the bishop and his clergy, whose task was to preserve the faith and take it to the surrounding countryside. Bishops had to be saints to lead such an enterprise. Their weapons were holiness and a simple lifestyle, together with the authority of their preaching. Bishops on thrones, behaving like kings, after the manner of feudal lands to the south, was never their way; neither the abbot nor the clergy and lay brothers would have allowed it. There was one palpable link with the Apostles that was left to them in their isolation, namely the Holy Scriptures. How jealously they guarded these. With what care and devotion they studied and copied them. A glance through the pages of the ancient Irish manuscripts or the Lindisfarne Gospels makes the point convincingly. The Celtic Church diverged from Rome. But it must be said that it also preserved some ingredients of the apostolic tradition that Rome had half forgotten.

The isolation and remoteness of the British Isles rather suited the Celtic temperament. For Celts it was instinctive to look for God in the world of nature. Mediterranean peoples saw the natural world as a threat to be subdued, but for the Celt there was inspiration in the wide open spaces, the rocky headlands, the pounding surf and the windswept moor. It made them very self-sufficient, and therefore rather good missionaries. Alone with God in a remote spot, with little fellowship and nothing in the way of creature comforts, they could manage quite nicely. They developed a missionary programme that took the Gospel effectively to the Anglo-Saxons settling in England as well as to much of northern Europe.

The Celtic style of Christianity left an indelible impression on the English mind. For the English, authentic Christianity has always been the sort lived and taught by giants of the faith like Aidan and Cuthbert – who clearly lived close to God and cared little for the comforts of this world, who taught powerfully from the Scriptures, but sought no worldly power beyond their ability to touch people's consciences by goodness and purity, and who were so sure of their message and of the love of God that they must go to the ends of the earth to tell of it. Ever since then the only preaching the English have ever really listened to is a Bible-based message, from a holy person, driven only by the love of God. Purity of ecclesiastical pedigree matters little to them as long as the life is right and the teaching is from the Scriptures. And they prefer it if the preacher is English.

However, the Celtic style of Christianity offers no way of continuing the Church when the giants have departed. When evangelism is over, what then? How do you build a consistent Christian presence in a community? It helps when the clergy are saints; but what is to be done when they are not? The Church needs first to be a school for sinners, or there will be no saints. Even Aidan and Cuthbert did not spring fully formed from a vacuum. There were communities of fumbling sinners, in those Irish fortresses that gave them birth; and now there was a need for the same sort of thing right across England.

The Church in every village
The Celtic Church in England only partly solved this problem. The completion of the task was left to Augustine with his band of well-organized workers from Rome; they slowly built up an ordered pattern that could continue for centuries even with indifferent leadership. Rome, of course, was right, but so were the Celts. The two styles were so different; somehow they had to resolve the tensions and the party-spirit that were damaging the Church's work. So they called the Synod of Whitby. It seemed to succeed, but in fact it failed miserably, for it turned its attention only to peripheral issues – so much easier to talk about than the deep underlying matters of the Spirit. How should they calculate the date of Easter? What form of tonsure should the clergy wear? It was not the last time that heated debate has centred on the Church calendar or clerical dress. Always such debates are fuelled by much deeper things that we would rather not bring into the open.

It was obvious that the English Church needed to come into line with the rest of Christendom; King Oswy made sure of that. And the saintly Bishop Cuthbert of Lindisfarne knew that this was the only way, and eventually backed the King. We had to be *catholic*. But the desire to be different in our own way persisted. Our ways too, and our methods of evangelism, had been greatly blessed by God and seemed true to Scripture. How could we forget them? So we wanted also to be *evangelical* – to use the term a later century would coin. Besides, the English are not a Mediterranean people, and we need to express our faith in the manner of our own culture and history. We wanted to do some things our own way without interference from abroad. It would be a full thirteen centuries before the Catholic Church generally would see the good sense of this, and allow a liturgy in English with English ways of doing it; some of us could not wait that long. If ever we felt manipulated by foreigners, or saw prelates from abroad lining their pockets at our expense, we would *protest*. Already we were *protestant* at heart. And if ever we thought that the Church in England was compromising the truth in an effort to preserve unity, we would refuse to *conform*, whatever the cost. Some of us were quite ready to be *nonconformist*, if we had to be.

But that is twentieth-century thinking. The seventh century needed uniformity and stability. Our time would like stability too; but we know that the only way is to live and let live. We have given up the awful delusion that truth can be established by force. At last we see the virtue of godly tolerance. We are aware of the vast world diversity of human cultures and historical patterns, and we see value in this variety. Television and foreign travel have transformed our attitudes to our fellow human beings. The Second Vatican Council, and the steady growing together of the Churches in our generation, have expanded our horizons and opened the way for new developments in Church relations. The possibility of being united but different is a heady dream that begins to haunt Christians all over the world. We have still to work out what it means.

The crumbling boundaries
It is hard now to realize how rigid were the barriers between the Churches in England until very recently. In the Suffolk village where I was brought up, Sunday morning saw the people moving in two opposing tides, the Church people towards the ancient village church to the sound of bells, the Chapel folk in the other direction summoned by a little thing that tinkled in the gable end of the Methodist Chapel; and some climbed the hill in silence to the Gospel Hall beyond. We, the Church of England people, had no idea what went on in the other places; and nobody talked about it. In a small community, discussion of such things was best avoided – though the men of the Gospel Hall would reprove anyone, from the squire down, heard swearing in public. We rather enjoyed this ritual response of theirs. It would always earn an apology, though without any apparent change of heart by the offender! The village boasted a handful of Roman Catholics, who would be seen climbing into a taxi, and going, we knew not whither, to attend Mass. The barriers were total and nobody saw any need to move them. It all seems worlds away now. Yet we thought of ourselves as a tolerant community; and compared with former generations so indeed we were. For the freedom of religion we accepted as normal was only finally won by catholics and dissenters in the last century.

Quite apart from these denominational barriers the Church of England had its own internal barriers, which were quite as rigid in their own way as those between the Churches. Each party in the Church of England ran its own theological colleges and maintained its own power base by acquiring the rights of presentation to key livings. There was little communication between the parties, and often very little trust.

In our time, however, the boundaries between the traditional styles of churchmanship have begun to blur. For centuries we were expert at signalling our differences to one another. As at Whitby, the signals were mostly to do with the calendar and clerical dress. Some kept saints' days, some ignored them. Some wore vestments, some did not. Not so long ago one glance as a man emerged from an Anglican vestry and you knew how he would take the service. The stereotypes were exact. You could tell at once whether he was a Celtic-style ascetic (an evangelical protestant), or a dressed-up imitator of Rome (an anglo-catholic, who refused even to be called a protestant) – or somewhere on the scale with its myriad gradations of high and low between these extremes. Even in the street the form of a clerical collar was enough to tell everything. But this has begun to change. We have evangelicals who wear vestments, not because they have 'gone broad', but from conviction. There are anglo-catholics who preach for a decision, like evangelicals. And the dog-collar, if it is worn at all, no longer reveals anything about party loyalties.

Indeed, clerical dress now reveals very little even about *denominational* loyalty. The real differences are often *within* the denominations rather than *between* them. There are catholics and evangelicals among the Methodists and URC; and they often find it easier to relate to their equivalents in the Church of England than to some in their own Churches. The development of Local Ecumenical Projects (LEPs) has shown how readily cross-denominational structures can now come into being; and these have played a wholesome part in forming new attitudes amongst English Christians generally. We are all beginning to discover new viewpoints from which to look at old controversies. And sometimes we then find that the differencies are matters of perspective rather than of reality, and that we have a unity in the underlying truths and experience we share that is wider than any one spiritual tradition. The doors are beginning to open, and we are all learning to explore ways of thinking that have been closed off to us for a long time.

But such a time as ours has its special dangers. Truth can easily be a casualty when ecumenical euphoria glows over everything. The only stability the Church will ever find is unity in *truth*. Our generation likes to think of truth as a matter of opinion. But for the Christian, truth is absolute, for it is defined in Christ; and the only way to find it is to live it out in the power of his Spirit.

Christians who claim to be catholic, protestant, evangelical, or non-conformist can now look afresh at each other and at the Roman Church from which we all sprang. We want room to be Celtic and Anglo-Saxon in the English Church; but we want also the strength and good order of the universal Church. Cuthbert was right: we dare not indefinitely part company with the rest of the Church. But we also value highly the insights and spirituality that history has bequeathed us; for we believe the hand of God has been in it. For many generations we have felt free to be independent and to follow our own vision. But now perhaps we are being called to renounce that independence, and embrace a deeper unity.

The frontier Church

At Whitby we avoided becoming a splinter Church. But we would always be the Church on the frontier; and this is a very different experience from being at the centre. Those in the Roman heartlands looked out on a world whose cultural patterns had a common origin; there was variety, but it was all familiar and well understood. At the frontier you spoke of things out there beyond the horizon; and this generated a different mental cast. We heard tales of strange people with unfamiliar ways. Who could say what you might find if you went out and looked for it?

It made for an adventurous spirit that was ready for anything. At the frontier all is open-ended, uncertain and exciting. The thought of being independent and doing your own thing without interference from the centre is never very far away; and, for a certain type of person, it is rather inviting. Protestantism, when it came in the sixteenth century, inevitably took root at the fringe of Christendom, and being a movement of independence it took a different form in each country. North Germany, Holland, Sweden, England, Scotland – each would develop its own form. And in each place, when eventually they learnt toleration, there would be room for a whole range of differing versions of the protestant culture.

Later we would export our religion to North America, Africa and the Far East; and with it would go all the variations we had generated. In their new homes around the world each new group of Christians would themselves claim the right to do their own thing without interference from anyone else. For the essence of protestantism is *independence*. In North America in particular the frontier spirit would rule supreme. 'Go west, young man'; and they did, millions of them, as the adventurous spirits of the world flocked to join in the fun. In that environment the spirit of protestantism flourished as never before.

Of course it could not go on like that; and the frontier spirit had its day. You may go west; but eventually you come to the Pacific Ocean. Sooner or later the last corner of the globe is charted and exploited, the last gold mine discovered, the last oil deposit tapped; and there is nowhere else to find adventure. The wisdom of the Almighty has set the human race to live on the surface of a sphere of limited area and of finite resources – just as he has given each of us a limited time-span and finite opportunities for enjoying it. There comes a point where to seek further adventure is to tread on someone else's toes; and that is unacceptable. The industrial world is full of enterprises trying to expand their business; but now, if you expand you probably make someone else bankrupt.

There is still adventure to be had, but it lies in a different direction. Now the excitement is in finding new science and economics for handling scarce resources, new politics for relating fruitfully to one another, new social structures to help us enjoy a multi-cultural world, and the moral basis for managing overcrowding with justice. The traditional sturdy independence of Anglo-Saxons (and many others) needs restraining; else blind self-interest will destroy us all. We have a very wise God, who gently but inexorably is forcing us to face a simple fact, namely that the world will run by the love he alone knows how to inspire, or not at all. We have a choice; but doing our own thing and being independent is not one of the options.

These pressures are operating on the Christian Church just as on the world at large. The protestant schism was a phase through which the Church probably had to pass; a certain independence of spirit was necessary if the Church was to emerge from the tangles of the Middle Ages and become God's instrument in the modern world. But that phase is ended. Protestants have contributed much to the world, and the Catholic Church may have some lessons still to learn from them; we return to that later. But the independence that stirs the hearts of so many protestants is a luxury we can no longer afford.

It is becoming more and more obvious that the real issues facing the world are moral and religious, but the world at large does not yet see this; it is convinced that the innate originality and drive of the human race will find the answers. New inventions, better communications, cleverer ways with money, greater international co-operation, and we will turn the corner: so present thinking runs. The secularism that dominates our world is not yet a played-out force, but one day humanity will need to look again at the Christian culture that offers an alternative to its own worn-out habits; and it will not be enough then for the Church to exhibit a range of competing Christian patterns that speak with a divided voice.

Thirteen centuries ago the followers of Cuthbert and Augustine found the grace to be united in the face of the pagan Anglo-Saxon culture. Thank God for that! So they could speak to us with the classic impact of Christ and his Apostles: 'The Kingdom of God is at hand.' And they could point to their own missionary communities and say: 'Come and see.' We must discover how to do that in our poor world that has forgotten how to be Christian.

There was unfinished business at Whitby: the Synod left behind things that would trouble the Church in later centuries. We shall look at these next. God has his own ways of curing blindness in his Church, and it is always a costly process. For unity in the Church can come only through the truth, and truth is never easily won, though obvious when you find it. We need to proceed at two levels. Some of the things that divide are trivial – as foolish as arguments about the calendar or clerical dress. But in other areas the only way forward is to look more deeply into the mystery of God, and seek to know him better; for that is the only way of finding the truth – and nothing is more difficult, or more rewarding! That is the adventure we must embark on.

2: THE ENGLISH CHURCH IN EUROPE

The English Church after Whitby was firmly integrated into Europe and the rest of the Church. The chief missionary instruments of the Church in England, as in the rest of Europe, were the monasteries. Increasingly they were of the Benedictine kind developed in southern Europe, rather than the Celtic sort derived from Ireland. The Benedictines worked to a common rule, and within a common architecture; when you arrived at a Benedictine house you knew where you were. Guests would be entertained carefully and well, and would be able to see in the deeply committed community a true example of Christian living. By contrast the Celtic monasteries were very diverse, and full of individualists. They were also terrifyingly ascetic; a guest would be looked after, but left in no doubt that the normal needs of the flesh were regarded as of little importance. This was their great strength in the missionary situation, working among pagans to whom the indulgence of the flesh came all too naturally. It produced some great saints, but it made them very hard to join; for the aspirant to the monastery had to embrace the style on a heroic scale. Most of us need to grow into Christian commitment over a period of time; and the Benedictine pattern provided a way in for ordinary people. So their monasteries grew and spread all over Christendom.

The English Church, therefore, acquired a completely European flavour. Anglo-Saxons and Celts, joined later by Normans, slowly grew into the English nation; and they did so with the Church at the heart of national consciousness. The other peoples of Europe – French, Spanish, German, and so on – also shared this experience of growing nationhood with the Church woven into the fabric of their national life. Where else could they look for their emerging needs of education, law, health and administration but to the Church? And the Benedictine monasteries were the engines of this development. This experience of the Church forming the stuff of our history is one we share with our partners in Europe, but with very few other countries in the world.

The English Church worldwide

Outside Europe it is different. In the English-speaking world and wherever else the English Church has spread, we have exported our protestantism and sense of independence, but not our special understanding of the Church as a national possession shared with Europe. These countries have other roots in the world and other links with the universal Church. Their national identity has been formed in different ways, and the strands of their Church life are drawn from many sources besides England. In the USA, for instance, with its diverse ethnic origins, the number of denominations seems beyond counting; and Christians there feel very little of the ecumenical pressure drawing the Churches together that we have experienced in England – a pressure most of us believe derives from the Holy Spirit.

The feeling of independence that most of the Anglican Communion regards as normal has not been an entirely helpful influence on the Church of England. It has made it think itself more significant on the world stage than it really is. For the Church of England consists of just two small provinces of the Western Church; and the whole of worldwide Anglicanism is only about 5 per cent of world Christianity. English eyes have focused for 400 years on distant parts of the world; and so we tend to see our place as out there and separate from Europe. But our future, like our past, spiritually as well as economically, is inevitably with Europe. It is in Europe, the old heart of Christendom, that Church unity is to be found. What we need is an expanded Europe that has room in its heart for the rest of the world.

The power struggles of Europe

It is strange that Europe has been the leader in developing the pattern of world civilization; for it has been as much rent by terrible wars, political oppressions and revolutions as any other region on earth. This did not hinder the growth and development of the Faith; for from its earliest years Christianity has shown itself well able to thrive in times of trouble and persecution. But maintaining the unity of Christendom has always been hard, with the secular states of Europe torn apart by wars and social unrest: and this was the task that the Western Church saw as the God-given role of the Bishops of Rome, the Popes. Amazingly, poor troubled Europe was the dynamic centre of Christianity, and will always be at the heart of its affairs. And amazingly, the unity of the Church depends still, as it has always done, on the papacy.

To fulfil this role Popes have to be men of high spiritual standing and ability; when they speak we need to hear the truth as it is in Jesus echoed in our hearts. To be free to do this Popes also need to be independent of the secular states in which the papacy is embedded, and this needs to be respected and protected by kings and rulers. We are familiar in our day with the concept of the Vatican living within its own walls, with a relationship of mutual respect with the encircling Italian state. But this arrangement dates only from 1930; for most of its history the papacy has had to struggle to be independent, and has rarely shown much wisdom in achieving it. Some Popes have had to flee from Rome; others have been prisoners for years within the Vatican, surrounded by enemies who could dictate their terms. Some have indeed shown courage in the face of political pressures, but very few have been free to act independently.

The setting of the Reformation

In the fourteenth and fifteenth centuries, leading up to the Reformation, the Popes were certainly not free and independent: the power struggles of the late Middle Ages made it quite impossible. Each emerging nation was still trying to carve out its own territory, and establish firm government within it; kings were proving their power against one other and against those in their own countries who were ready to snatch it from them. The Hundred Years War was fought over the English kings' claim to the French throne. It eventually petered out in about 1450; the French kings then had the task of asserting their authority against their Burgundian rivals. The English kings too were caught up in their own dynastic struggles, the Wars of the Roses. Both nations, however, eventually achieved strong government.

The German states, by contrast, failed to find any political unity in that period. Traditionally the Holy Roman Emperor held the reins in central Europe, but at that time he was unable to make his leadership effective against the petty rulers of the German states. The Spanish peninsula was at first divided into three kingdoms; one of these for a time also held sovereignty over Sicily and southern Italy. The Spanish kingdom became united only in the latter half of the fifteenth century; but they then also established strong and effective government. Italy, however, would remain for many centuries a patchwork of competing and warring states.

Within this pattern of ceaseless conflict the papacy was struggling to survive – trying to gain some sort of independence from the worldly powers that threatened to engulf it or coerce it to serve their own interests. Also it needed revenues on which to live and function effectively; only so could it maintain its quite proper role in the Church it existed to serve and unify. But the European rulers were hard pressed to raise taxation for their own internecine wars, and usually resisted attempts to divert precious resources to the papacy. It would have been wonderful if the Popes had found the grace to embrace a self-denying poverty and asceticism after the style of St Francis – to rule Christendom by a Christ-like example and the power of a holy life. There were fine Christians in Europe who might have done it; but they were not likely to be elected Pope.

So the Popes were caught up in the same power struggle as all the other rulers, and were driven to use the same sorts of worldly methods to achieve their aims. They fielded powerful armies, and engaged in the most worldly diplomacy. They also wielded weapons not available to others. The blessing (or the condemnation) of a Pope was a powerful political tool, often used effectively. The power of appointment to lucrative ecclesiastical posts was an even more potent weapon, and could be used for fund raising – such posts had a way of going to the highest bidder. This was potentially so subversive that kings and rulers were forced to resist it; for in an age when administration was in the hands of clerics, antagonistic clergy could well undermine the government of the country. Kings always made sure that bishops and abbots were people they could live with. Indeed they went further and usually chose for these posts people who would be useful in government – and these duly became ministers of the Crown and civil servants. Whether from the Crown or the Pope top Church appointments were very remunerative, and the system ensured that those who benefited had an interest in keeping it that way. Corruption in the Church was endemic, an open scandal all over Christendom. But neither kings nor Popes, who had the power to make changes, had an interest in doing so.

There were protests, particularly in the newly founded universities, who enjoyed some freedom of expression. But most people just felt helpless and angry, and anti-clerical feeling was rife. Sooner or later the bubble would burst, and great harm would be done.

The English Community Church

In spite of the corruption that degraded much of the Church hierarchy, we must recognize that the local Church in England (as in much of Europe) was very much alive. There were many faithful parish priests who fulfilled their role within their limits. They might be very poor, for the funds available were siphoned off to others. They were often badly educated, which was not their fault. But they served a community with a throbbing spirituality that affected every area of life; and, as always, to be in such a position is itself no mean reward. Looking back from a later century there were foolish and unbalanced things going on, things that we must call superstitious. But in the terms of their culture the strength and vitality of Church life in England in the early sixteenth century was of a very high order. There was a total community involvement that is hard to imagine in our day; and there was a thriving devotional life, as the primers and prayer books for private use clearly show. Yes, they wanted an end to corruption in the Church. But above all they just wanted to be left alone to do their own Church thing in their own way – just as English congregations had always done, and still do to this day.

Indeed much of the popular pressure that was bound sooner or later to bring reformation derived from the teaching success of the Church in earlier centuries. People understood very clearly the ethical demands of the Faith; and they knew that these applied not only to the man and woman in the pew but to the high-ups in the Church too. They could smell corruption, and felt betrayed when nothing was done about it. Their own friends in the Church seemed truer examples of Christian living than many of the bishops who lorded it over them. Private conscience seemed a better guide to behaviour than the teaching to be heard from such hypocrites. So the spirit of protestantism was fostered. The Gospel of Christ quite rightly generated a strong egalitarian feeling, which would increasingly resent the inequalities of wealth and privilege that the system supported. Justice was a concept that Christian people had learnt to value.

There were of course some people articulate enough to give expression to such feelings. There was John Wycliffe in Oxford in the late fourteenth century. As an academic he wrote in learned and measured Latin, and challenged the right of corrupt men to rule the Church. But he also prompted the first attempt to translate the Bible into English.

The people should have the Scriptures in their own language, he said, so they could decide for themselves what was the true teaching. But Wycliffe's reasoning seemed to challenge *all* authority, secular as well as clerical; and this was seen as seditious. His followers were pursued as rebels against the king; or they might be dealt with as heretics – it made little difference in that century. University support was withdrawn, and the movement continued only underground, where ordinary people met to read the Bible and ponder it together. But most people had little sympathy with the Lollards, as they were called: there seemed no room for them within the crowded framework of ordinary parish life.

Similar movements arose in many parts of Europe. Some were persecuted, some operated with a measure of official support. Some led to the forming of new kinds of religious communities; and these played a part in generating the attitudes that would eventually transform the Church. New Renaissance thinking was flowing out from Italy into the universities all over Europe, as well as into the homes of the increasing class of people with some education. The ancient cultures of Greece and Rome were being looked at again; old manuscripts were coming to light, and the Bible was being studied in Greek and Hebrew, along with the writings of the early Church Fathers. Printing was making documents of all kinds available in a way they had never been before. People were asking themselves what the Gospels and the Letters of St Paul had meant to those who first read them; and there were able men in the land who could begin to give the answers. In London, John Colet was appointed Dean of St Paul's, and astonished many with the simplicity and directness of his expositions of the Letters of St Paul, the young future King Henry VIII among them.

Christendom in fragments

Until the sixteenth century nobody imagined that reformation required any real break with the past. What we needed was reform of the structures of the Church and a break with corruption. There was a growing appreciation of our ancient Christian heritage, and no thought of trying to build a separate Church. The papacy was valued as a focus of unity for the Church, and as an ultimate court of appeal, even when there was little respect for the particular holder of the office – and certainly no intention of allowing him any significant control of affairs in our own country. The leaders of Church and State in Europe tried everything to achieve reform. They called General Councils, to force the hands of the Church hierarchy; the body of Cardinals (who elect Popes) tried to act on their own initiative and depose Popes who would not bring in reform. At one stage this led to no fewer than three Popes, none of whom recognized the legality of the others.

The kings of Europe had the power to force the pace, but could not agree on how to do it; none of them dare risk destabilizing the fragile political life of his own country. Only in Spain was reform forced through and corruption largely stamped out. Here the pressing need was to unite the country as a single Christian monarchy; for part of it (Granada) was still under the control of Muslims. The Muslims and the Jews, there and in other parts of Spain, had lived happily alongside their Christian neigh-bours for centuries with mutual respect and toleration. But all this ceased when Granada was finally conquered in 1492; and the tolerant tradition of centuries was overthrown. The Muslims and the Jews were then either expelled or else forcibly 'converted'. Such a harsh and dreadful policy could only be carried through if the Christian Church in Spain was con-strained into an absolutely single-minded orthodoxy. All deviation from this was therefore ruthlessly put down. It brought reform to Spain, but at what a cost! And it meant that the hard line of the Spanish Church would rule the day in southern Europe when reform was eventually forced on the rest of the Church by the Lutheran rebellion.

Whether reform would ever have come if Luther had not nailed his theses to the door of Wittenberg church is a debatable point. The theses themselves were rather abstruse and not really seditious; Luther had no thought at that stage of breaking up the Church. But one thing led to another, and before long separation from Rome was the only policy he could pursue. Fortunately for Luther the weakness and division of the German states allowed him to get away with it; and his act of defiance kindled the fire of popular anti-clerical grievances. For the first time it became possible to imagine a separate Church, with its own centres of authority owing nothing to the Pope. Elsewhere in Europe government was strong enough to keep the separatist tendency of protestantism in check. In France and Spain the State continued to accept the Pope as head. Religious wars would come, but would be contained. The same would no doubt have happened in England, for Henry VIII was very firmly in the saddle of power and had no use for the deviations from catholicism he perceived in Luther's theology.

The English compromise
However, Henry VIII was desperate for a male heir; so was all England, which had had quite enough of dynastic struggles in the Wars of the Roses. Catherine, the wife he had inherited from his deceased brother Arthur, was clearly unable to oblige. Henry needed a divorce – or, more

precisely, an annulment, for surely his youthful marriage to his brother's wife was illegal and invalid, whatever may have been said at the time? But the Pope just then was under the control of the Emperor Charles V, whose armies had recently occupied Rome; and Catherine was Charles's aunt and a princess of Aragon in his dominions. So the Pope delayed a decision on Henry's petition. It seemed intolerable that English State affairs should be subject to the court intrigues of distant Mediterranean lands, and Henry set about ending all papal control over the English Church. Henceforth the king in parliament would be supreme, in Church as in State.

Henry VIII certainly never intended setting up a new religion. His book in opposition to Lutheran theology had earned him from the Pope the title 'Defender of the Faith' – a title that still appears (as F.D.) on our coinage. He continued for many years after the break to burn protestants as heretics; he also beheaded catholics who refused to renounce papal supremacy. His apparent intention was to retain everything in the Church just as it had always been, but with himself at the head of it instead of the Pope. But the logic of the situation drove him and his successors by slow degrees into an eventual partnership with the out-and-out protestants. Henry, and later his daughter Elizabeth I, demanded a sacramental religion; and they would both have preferred to continue with an unmarried priesthood. They gave way on that point, provided they could curb clerical power; for the only power in the country must be that of the Sovereign. So they stripped the Church Convocations of their traditional power. Also they rooted out superstitious practices which gave unscrupulous clergy power over people's minds. But beyond these they hoped to leave things as they were.

Popular support for Henry VIII came from the anti-clerical feeling that seethed beneath the surface. When the Tudors unleashed this force, they released also a godless greed; and before long, everyone from the monarch down would be helping themselves to the assets of the Church, the social and religious heritage of the English people for over a thousand years. Inevitably the Tudors were forced into an alliance with the protestants, who longed for nothing more than to see all these ancient things swept away, along with images in churches and anything else that reminded them of a past they detested. Before many years Henry and his successors would be using the full apparatus of Tudor state coercion to strip the churches of the land, and to force on the English people a pattern of religion that was alien to their ways.

Why did the English people allow it? First, they wanted peace. All over Europe there were bloody religious wars and conflicts; and they wanted none of it. Then, as protestantism took hold in England the catholic powers of Europe set their sights on destroying Elizabeth and imposing a catholic government. So there was a lot to be said for the strong Tudor monarchs, who successfully kept England from foreign domination. When the Pope excommunicated Elizabeth in 1570, inviting her catholic subjects to turn against her, there were not many who responded, even in their hearts; but the action made loyal English catholics look like foreign subversives – an image they retained for several centuries.

The protestants had created a new religion, which was built up out of ingredients from the old, but selected in such a way as to form a barrier against all that might draw people back to the old catholic faith and practice. Protestantism would survive only if that barrier stayed intact. But Elizabeth finally left a time-bomb within the system, for she refused to go all the way with the protestants. The Church of England would retain its Orders of Ministry – its bishops, priests, and deacons – and its sacraments, and with them its claim to be still part of the ancient Catholic Church of the land. The Tudors and their parliament created for the Church of England a *sacramental protestantism*, a typical English compromise, which would ever afterwards be pulling the Church of England in opposite directions. Were we catholic, or were we protestant? Each person answered it in his or her own way. But most just went on being English.

3: A NEW RELIGION

Reformation had been in the air for at least 150 years before anyone suggested a break with Rome. Even Luther, who engineered that first rupture, originally had no thought of setting up a separate Church. The Reformers in every country were looking rather for a *renewed* religion – a religion that would impinge on the hearts and lives of the people, and be much more than a mere external performing of the right ceremonies. They hoped this would lead to a new simplicity of lifestyle at all levels of society; and they were affronted by the corruption among the higher clergy that was a denial of all true religion, and negated their own efforts at reform. But they had every intention of continuing the same religion inherited from ancient time; and they meant to stay in the one Catholic Church, with its orders of bishops, priests and deacons, presided over by the Pope as the bishop of Rome.

However, when Luther challenged the iniquitous money-raising system sanctioned by the Pope he challenged the Pope's authority. Deny the system, and you deny the authority that backs the system; and you are then looking around for another authority on which to base the life of the Church. Remove the Pope, and you then have the problem of whom or what to put in his place. Indeed the whole system then needs re-structuring and re-thinking on a new foundation. All Christians can agree that Christ is the Head of the Church. But there are practical decisions to be made, and we have to be clear what is the ultimate court of appeal for the Church here on earth. Protestants have spent the last 450 years trying to resolve that problem, using kings, councils, parliaments, assemblies, synods, and so on. Protestant Churches all have their official constitutions; but who sanctions the constitutions? *The people*, our democratic generation answers; but do *they* have some divine right denied to Popes and kings?

In the sixteenth century the power to re-structure the Church rested in practice with the local secular authority, the city council or the local ruler. For many centuries the authority of the Pope had extended deep into the financial and administrative life of every country in Christendom. There was no sinister plot in this; it was just the way things had worked best for a very long time. Luther's revolt was an attempt to break the secular power of the Pope; he would have liked to leave his spiritual power intact. But with an unwilling Pope, breaking one kind of power involved dealing with the other kind too. Only the State had the practical muscle to do that.

The new approach to authority also demanded a new theology of the Church: what was a Church without a Pope? If you remove the Pope, how much else has to go too? Do you have bishops? Or priests? Or sacraments? What exactly now is the ministry of the Church? Who has authority to teach? And from whom is it derived? Who can be trusted to give correct teaching, and how do we know what is right and what is wrong? Protestants had to look for the answers to these questions in the Bible; for this was the only possible weapon with which to refute a Pope. How the Bible was deployed in this struggle depended on the spiritual discernment of the leaders involved; and this in turn depended, far more than protestants have usually been prepared to recognize, on the temperament and background of those leaders.

Luther was by temperament a traditionalist, and when the break came he was no longer young. The Church must be ruled by the Bible; and that meant for him that traditional practices could continue unless the Bible definitely forbade them. So the Lutheran Church continued with a sacramental pattern little altered from the past, and used eucharistic vestments, sang hymns, and expected to make private confessions. The Swiss Reformers, when they joined the revolt against the Pope, saw it all differently; for them nothing was to happen in church unless it was *positively* required by the Bible. So their worship tended to simplicity, with no vestments and no hymns (only metrical psalms); and they discouraged private confessions.

It was not long before northern Europe was full of competing protestant denominations, each interpreting the Scriptures in its own way, and only partly in fellowship with one another. Some Churches retained much of the inherited pattern of ministry and sacraments; others stripped away most of these things.

The Church of England

The Church of England was perhaps extreme in seeking to preserve the traditional orders and sacraments almost in their entirety. The only change was the substitution of the king in parliament for the Pope as its ultimate authority. In the local church people hardly noticed the difference. The goings-on of those in charge, whether at Westminster or Rome, were all in another world from theirs – until, that is, some new thing was imposed on them by the powers that be. It is the same with the modern General Synod; few people are aware of its debates – until it does something that affects local church life. And then the reaction is the same as in the Tudor Church: dumb resentment. The people do not like it, but are not prepared to make trouble in the Church.

For *local* Christians the Church must have *continuity*; its worship and the conduct of its affairs must follow the pattern hallowed by the centuries. They need to feel they are sharing in the Christian life and discipleship known to their ancestors. They know there must be change and development; but this should be by organic growth out of the old, not by a discontinuous imposition from outside. All sudden change will be seen in the local church as fundamentally false and irreligious. But reformers – in every generation – never seem to realize this.

The Tudor Church was allowed no such quiet organic evolution. The whole pattern of local church life was altered out of all recognition in the space of one generation. They had to endure the wholesale eviction of the saints from their churches and their calendars. No longer were they to be allowed the sense of our Lord reigning with his saints over the world and over their community in particular. No longer were they to be reminded of the cost of their redemption by the rood that filled the chancel arch; such things must now be in the mind and in the heart; and those with poor imaginations found it hard to focus. No longer was the Lord present in the sacrament on the altar or in the pyx above it; for now they were taught that he was present only in the heart of the believer who received the sacrament – and that only for a believer in a state of grace. The altar was removed from the place towards which the whole church architecture pointed, and replaced by an ordinary table in the nave – and the word 'altar' itself was banished from the Prayer Book. The priest was no longer the special representative of Christ; he was another member of the congregation dressed in plain clothes, and given a new service to recite. The old familiar Mass was banned.

It was a new religion, and they knew it. However, the real protestants in England were never satisfied with the Tudor settlement. For them it was a messy compromise that left in place too many links with the old Church. They did not believe in priests at all, and wanted to abolish the very word. The sacraments they saw as no more than aids to faith, not vehicles of the grace of God. They wanted a heart religion with no external aids – except the word of God. The Tudors never went far enough for them. Many eventually left to form the nonconformist denominations. But others stayed in the national Church as the best arena in which to work, hoping to move it gradually in a more protestant direction; their heirs are to be found in the present evangelical party of the Church of England.

Of course no protestant has ever accepted the charge of introducing a new religion. They claim to have gone back to the true *old* religion, as the Lord and his Apostles gave it, before the corrupting effects of later papal power. They see the Catholic Church, and the Popes of the Middle Ages in particular, as the ones who introduced the *new* things. The Catholic Church, they say, by incorporating later Church additions, has distorted the true Faith; and they want to get back to the *original faith of the Apostles as found in Scripture*. Whichever side is right, one thing is quite certain: the Catholic Faith and the Protestant Faith are two different religions. They both share allegiance to Jesus Christ as Lord, and accept the Bible as the set of foundation documents of the Church; so the two religions have much in common, as our generation is at last discovering. But they work in different ways, and that is what we have to understand and explore.

Scripture only
The over-riding objective of the first protestant reformers was to free the Church from the control of priests, for in their perception it was through the priesthood that the Pope exercised his control of the Church. They needed to rid the Church of priests; then there would be

no Pope and no bishops, and no one making themselves rich on Church revenues. The only way of banishing priests from the system was to go back to the Bible, and forbid all Church doctrine and practice that emerged after the age of the Apostles. For within a generation of that time Church leaders were writing in their letters about priests and bishops very much in the terms we use today; the vocabulary was different – they did not use the word 'priest' – but they meant the same as we do. The early Church Fathers seemed to assume that this Church structure was implicit in the instructions left them by the Apostles. If we once allow that the first post-apostolic Church was being guided into all truth by the Holy Spirit, then we have to accept the orders of bishops, priests and deacons as part of the Lord's will for his Church; and this protestants could not do. So they were obliged to insist on *Scripture only* as the basis of the Church. To them all subsequent developments were suspect and disposable.

This insistence on Scripture only is both the strength and the weakness of the protestant approach. It is a strength in that the foundations of their position are very clearly marked out by the limits of the Old and New Testaments. Also it leads protestants to study the Bible with great seriousness and at great depth; for here is everything they want to know. The Church of the Middle Ages failed seriously through its widespread ignorance of the Bible. Whatever other truth the Church may subsequently have been led into, the Bible was always foundational, and should never have been neglected. Would that the Roman Catholic Church of today were more definite on this point! The official teaching is clear enough; and the liturgy and offices of the Church make full use of the Bible. But the Bible is still not seen generally as a vital ingredient of personal devotional life.

However, to insist on Scripture only is also a great weakness in the protestant position, for it implies that the Church started going off the rails as soon as the last Apostle died. With the memory of the Apostles' teaching ringing in their ears, already Church leaders, the protestants claim, were introducing practices for which they had no warrant; and this situation got steadily worse down the centuries – until Luther and his fellow Reformers came on the scene and restored things to their pristine beauty! Are we to believe that the Church of Christ went through some 1,500 years of gross error until the protestants came along? Modern protestants usually put it more charitably: 'In spite of the false system', they say, 'during those 1,500 years there were many true Christians in the Church.' But that will not do either. Surely our Lord's presence in his Church is more immediate and definite than that!

There will always be weeds appearing in his field, but there is also the good seed that bears a crop for eternal life; these are the ones who have heard his call, and witness in every generation faithfully to their Lord, and so carry forward the tradition of his Church.

In point of fact the Church went off the rails frequently even during the time of the Apostles. Their letters were usually written to correct some serious error. But our Lord promised that 'the gates of Hades will not overcome' his Church (Matt 16:18); and we have to believe that he knew what he was doing. He used the Apostles, in person and by letter, to correct the Church – just as he has used Church leaders in every generation since. The Church, protestant or catholic, will always be going wrong and needing correcting, and the good Lord will always find ways of doing it. If the Church does not listen and remains obstinate against him, it will inevitably fall into schism; for it can only hold together in truth. When truth is ignored the Church must split.

There have been other schisms in the history of the Church; the most important was that between the Eastern Churches (the Orthodox) and the Western Church (led by the Pope). This schism is limping slowly towards a resolution, but it still exerts a damaging effect on the worldwide Church; for it seems to provide two competing centres for Christians seeking to return to the ancient disciplines of the Church. It seems to offer a choice, where there should be just the ancient Church of Christ. Christians in England should historically be drawn to the Western Church; but our world is now so cosmopolitan that many English Christians face great difficulties of conscience at this point, deciding which of the two ancient Churches they should approach.

Schism is the worst disaster into which human sin can drive the Church. Almost always the fault is on both sides. The two part company, each claiming to bear true witness to Christ. In fact the witness of the whole Church is impaired and faulty until they are together again; and to this place of repentance and renewal the Lord will eventually move them. The way there is through listening to each other; then they may eventually hear what the good Lord too is saying to them. I am not quite sure that the Catholic Church (outside its leadership) has yet learnt the full lesson of the Reformation; so the protestants may still have a job of witness to do – but perhaps not for long. And at least some protestants are now hearing the call to come home, and they are hearing it as an absolute imperative over-riding all else. There can be no place in the end for a *second* Christian religion.

THE PRIESTLY
PRESENCE
The catholic challenge to protestants

Away with the notion that good shepherds are lacking at present; let us
not entertain the idea; may the Lord's mercy never fail to produce and
appoint them. Surely if there are good sheep, there are good shepherds
too, for good shepherds are made from good sheep . . . it is Christ who
feeds them. . . . So let them all be in the one shepherd, and speak with the
one shepherd's voice. . . . Let the sheep hear this voice, cleared of all division and cleansed of all heresy, and let them follow their shepherd as he
says, 'Those who are my sheep hear my voice and follow me'.

St Augustine of Hippo, fifth century, *Sermon* 46, 29–30

4: PRIESTS IN THE CHURCH

Protestants have difficulties with priesthood. The main objective of
their theology has always been to dispense with the concept of priesthood altogether. They would prefer to describe those authorized to celebrate the Eucharist, and to bless and absolve in Christ's name, by the
New Testament name *presbyter* or *elder*. They do not believe that the
Church has *priests* who alone can validly do these things; nor do they see
a need for priests to act as mediators between us and God, since Christ
alone is that, and all Christians have direct access to God through him.
'For there is one God and one mediator between God and men, the man
Christ Jesus' (1 Tim 2:5). All believers are priests, they say, and none can
be set apart in a ministerial priesthood. St Peter was addressing the *whole*
people of God when he wrote 'You are a chosen people, a royal priesthood, a holy nation, a people belonging to God' (1 Peter 2:9).

They acknowledge that good order in the Church requires those who
preside at the Lord's Table to be properly authorized to do so. But they
do not recognize their *priesthood* in some special sense – beyond the
priesthood of all believers. They would be happy, in principle, to see a
lay person presiding at the Eucharist. Much of the debate about women
priests has been meaningless to evangelicals in the Church of England,
since if all believers, male and female alike, are already priests – in the

only sense in which they recognize that word – then why argue whether women can be priests: they are that already, along with every other believer. But is this what the priesthood of all believers really implies?

It has always amazed me that the rest of the Church never really tries to counter such evangelical reasoning. We point to history and the Church Fathers as authority for an order of priests, but we never deploy the one sort of argument that evangelicals might recognize – an argument from Scripture. So let us for once do just that: make a case *from Scripture* for an order of priests set apart in the Church.

The priest as a bridge-person

First let us be quite clear what a priest is – in any religion. A priest is a bridge-person, who stands between God and the world, a mediator who represents the one to the other, and provides communication between them. To the world the priest represents God and speaks for him. To God the priest represents the world, holding before him the needs of the people, and making their offerings to him.

The Old Testament priesthood was limited to those of the tribe of Levi descended from Aaron, the first High Priest of the people of Israel. This priesthood was superseded by our Lord's sacrificial offering of himself on the cross. The Letter to the Hebrews makes this point. It quotes Psalm 110 as a designation applying to Christ: 'The Lord has sworn and will not change his mind, "You are a priest for ever, in the order of Melchizedek"' (Ps 110:4). Melchizedek was a mysterious priest-king of Jerusalem in the days of Abraham (Gen 14:18). We know nothing of his origins, nor of his end; and the writer of the Letter to the Hebrews sees this as like Jesus – coming out of eternity, and returning to eternity, and the source of a new order of priesthood, replacing the old priesthood of Aaron.

> If perfection could have been attained through the Levitical priest-hood (for on the basis of it the law was given to the people), why was there still need for another priest to come – one in the order of Melchizedek, not in the order of Aaron? (Heb 7:11)

The old priesthood was thus shown to be inadequate and capable only of pointing forward to the true high-priesthood of Christ, an eternal priesthood he exercises on behalf of all humanity.

> Because Jesus lives for ever, he has a permanent priesthood. There-fore he is able to save completely those who come to God through

him, because he always lives to intercede for them. Such a high priest meets our need – one who is holy, blameless, pure, set apart from sinners, exalted above the heavens. (Heb 7:24–26)

There is clearly no place any longer for the sacrificial priesthood of the Old Testament. Instead we have the priesthood to which the Old Testament pattern pointed, the eternal high-priesthood of Christ. This, like its forerunner, is also a sacrificial priesthood, the sacrificial offering being none other than Christ himself.

He did not enter by means of the blood of goats and calves; but he entered the Most Holy Place once for all by his own blood, having obtained eternal redemption. The blood of goats and bulls and the ashes of a heifer sprinkled on those who are ceremonially unclean sanctify them so that they are outwardly clean. How much more, then, will the blood of Christ, who through the eternal Spirit offered himself unblemished to God, cleanse our consciences from acts that lead to death, so that we may serve the living God! For this reason Christ is the mediator of a new covenant, that those who are called may receive the promised eternal inheritance – now that he has died as a ransom to set them free from the sins committed under the first covenant. (Heb 9:12–15)

He is both the priest, who represents the whole human race before the Father, and the offering whose life is offered for the life of the world. His offering of himself to God on the cross was perfect. Nothing can be added to it; and it need never be repeated, for it is totally sufficient to save the whole world. This is unlike the old priesthood of Aaron and its pattern of sacrifices, which brought about no enduring holiness.

The law is only a shadow of the good things that are coming – not the realities themselves. For this reason it can never by the same sacrifices repeatedly endlessly year after year, make perfect those who draw near to worship. If it could, would they not have stopped being offered? (Heb 10:1–2)

So our Lord Jesus Christ brings into the world a new sort of priesthood, with a new sort of sacrifice, through which he imparts to human beings a holiness like his own.

He sets aside the first to establish the second. And by that will, we have been made holy through the sacrifice of the body of Jesus Christ once for all. (Heb 10:9–10)

The Catechism of the Catholic Church sums it up like this:

> Everything that the priesthood of the Old Covenant prefigured finds its fulfilment in Christ Jesus, the 'one mediator between God and men'. The Christian tradition considers Melchizedek, 'priest of God Most High', as a prefiguration of the priesthood of Christ, the unique 'high priest after the order of Melchizedek'; 'holy, blameless, unstained', 'by a single offering he has perfected for all time those who are sanctified', that is, by the unique sacrifice of the cross. (CCC 1544)

Christ's priesthood shared

The question we must now consider is this: How much of Christ's priesthood does he share with us, his people? The general New Testament principle is that he came to give himself totally to us – to share with us all that he is and has. He shared our human life, in order that we might share his divine life. Does this include his priesthood? And to what extent does it include it? Is there anything of himself that our Lord does not share with us?

It is a fundamental of Christian teaching that the Son of God became a human being in order to share with humanity the riches of his divinity.

> For you know the grace of our Lord Jesus Christ, that though he was rich, yet for your sakes he became poor, so that you through his poverty might become rich. (2 Cor 8:9)

His love, his joy and obedience to the Father (John 15:9–11), his peace (John 14:27), his wisdom (John 16:13–15), and every other quality that is his as the incarnate Son of God he shares with us, so that we might be loving, joyful, obedient, at peace with the world and with ourselves, and filled with his wisdom for life. He even bequeathed to us a share in his risen life, which he won for us all on Easter Day; and so he shares with us his eternal life (John 17:2), a quality of life that starts now and will continue in his presence for ever (John 17:24).

But he also went on to share with humanity the ministry and commission he himself had received from the Father. He shared this first with the Apostles, and then through them with the growing Church; and to bring this into effect he bequeathed to them his Spirit. '"As the Father has sent me, I am sending you." And with that he breathed on them and said, "Receive the Holy Spirit"' (John 20:21–22). By so doing he shared with them also his priesthood, and we must explore what this implies. But first we must note that there is one aspect of his work which he cannot and does not share with us: his atoning death on the cross. This was a lonely task that he undertook by himself: he endured the ultimate penalty for human sin in order that we might never have to. He experienced the outer darkness of separation so that this might never be our lot. He alone could make that ultimate sacrificial offering to God, and be himself the ultimate sacrificial victim. At this point there is no sharing, but rather substitution. He took our place, and bore the burden of our sin so that we might be free of it. All we can do is believe it and receive by faith with thanksgiving the benefits he has won for us.

God made him who had no sin to be sin for us, so that in him we might become the righteousness of God. (2 Cor 5:21)

Christ redeemed us from the curse of the law by becoming a curse for us, for it is written: 'Cursed is everyone who is hanged on a tree.' He redeemed us in order that the blessing given to Abraham might come to the Gentiles through Christ Jesus, so that by faith we might receive the promise of the Spirit. (Gal 3:13–14)

In offering himself to the Father, our Lord was also offering to God the whole of the human race, with whom he identified. By grace every one of us is invited to take our part in this offering of humanity to God – and for Christ's sake the offer is accepted. Our lives, worthless in themselves, are caught up in his great self-offering; and so we too may give our lives alongside him in order to continue his priestly service to the world.

The one who died on the cross was a *perfect* being with no sin of his own; and the sacrifice he offered was a perfect offering. He was also an *eternal* being, eternally present, so that the work done there on the cross would be always a present reality and always effective in reconciling sinful humanity to God. What Christ achieved on Calvary was thus written into the innermost fabric of the universe. We live in a universe in which sinful beings may be reconciled to God through his action in Christ at one particular point in space-time – on Calvary under Pontius Pilate – and in which struggling human beings may offer their lives to God and find the offer accepted. In Christ the kingdom of God is at hand.

Vehicles of the Gospel

The benefits Christ gained for us we receive by faith through the Gospel sacraments. In baptism we die to sin and rise again to new life.

> We died to sin; how can we live in it any longer? Or don't you know that all of us who were baptized into Christ Jesus were baptized into his death? We were therefore buried with him through baptism into death in order that, just as Christ was raised from the dead through the glory of the Father, we too might live a new life. If we have been united with him in his death, we will certainly also be united with him in his resurrection. For we know that our old self was crucified with him so that the body of sin might be rendered powerless, that we should no longer be slaves to sin – because anyone who has died has been freed from sin. (Rom 6:2–7)

In the Holy Communion we bring our flawed lives to him, and receive instead the nourishment of his risen life.

> For the bread of God is he who comes down from heaven and gives life to the world. . . . I am the living bread that came down from heaven. If a man eats of this bread, he will live for ever. This bread is my flesh, which I will give for the life of the world. . . . I tell you the truth, unless you eat the flesh of the Son of Man and drink his blood, you have no life in you. Whoever eats my flesh and drinks my blood has eternal life, and I will raise him up at the last day. . . . Just as the living Father sent me and I live because of the Father, so the one who feeds on me will live because of me. This is the bread that came down from heaven. (John 6:33, 51, 53–54, 57–58)

When we obey his command 'Do this in memory of me' it is far more than a mere recollection of what he did for us: it is a partaking in his saving work by faith, by which we receive our share in the salvation he wrought for us, and are able to contribute our share in the offering of Christ to the Father.

Both these sacraments depend entirely on the saving work of Christ in his death and resurrection. There is an organic link between that saving work and the sacraments; they exist together in the same universe, so that the sacraments make available the saving work of Christ. To receive the sacraments faithfully is to receive the ongoing forgiveness of God and the growing blessing of the new life in Christ. To offer the sacraments is to play our part in the endless self-offering of humanity to the Father. When the Church celebrates and shares the sacraments, it is playing its part in the priesthood of Christ in the way he ordained. There is now no other priesthood than that of Christ. When we talk of the priesthood of all believers, it is the priesthood Christ shared with us that we are referring to; there can be no other.

In Christ's place

As we have said, a priest is a bridge-person, standing between God and the world. Our Lord Jesus Christ is the only mediator between God and humanity, the only bridge, the only priest; but he shares that role with us. When we offer to the world, by word and sacrament, the new life in Christ, we are exercising the priesthood of Christ; we are part of the bridge. When we intercede for the world in Christ's name, our prayers are part of his continual priestly intercession. When we celebrate the Eucharist we proclaim to the world the Lord's death until he comes (1 Cor 11:26); we also present before God the eternally present sacrifice of his Son as the ground of our forgiveness and blessing, and the means of offering our lives to him in matching love and obedience. And so we play our part in making effective the priestly ministry of Christ. The Eucharist adds nothing to what Christ has already done; but it makes it powerfully effective among us. The Eucharist is therefore at the heart of the Gospel proclamation, and the priest is at the place where the power of the Gospel is made available. As the Catechism of the Catholic Church puts it:

> The redemptive sacrifice of Christ is unique, accomplished once for all; yet it is made present in the Eucharistic sacrifice of the Church. The same is true of the one priesthood of Christ; it is made present through the ministerial priesthood without diminishing the unique-ness of Christ's priesthood: 'Only Christ is the true priest, the others being only his ministers.' (CCC 1545)

The priest exercises the priesthood of all believers, which is the priesthood of Christ. But this leads us on to a further point: are only some called to the priestly ministry centred on the Eucharist, as catholic tradition maintains? Or does the priesthood of all believers imply that all equally are entitled to perform the priestly role at the Eucharist?

5: PRIESTS SET APART

The argument between protestants and catholics about priesthood is rather like the argument about infant baptism. If you examine the New

Testament alone, the case for *infant* baptism looks a poor one; at best it remains unproved. But consider the *whole* Bible, and it is much more convincing; bring in also the evidence of the early Church Fathers, and the case is overwhelming. Entry into the benefits of the Old Covenant was by the rite of circumcision, administered when children were eight days old; it was an act of God's grace, requiring faithfulness on the part of parents and community, but not dependent on the decision of the child. Later they might reject their place within the covenant; but for the time being children unquestionably belonged to the community of faith. This was the setting, deriving from God himself, within which the early Church emerged.

When a child was born among them, how could they be more restrictive under the New Covenant than under the Old? Without doubt those early Jewish Christians both administered circumcision on the eighth day, and baptized children to incorporate them into Christ. The whole cultural pattern demanded it. It must have been done at least with the tacit approval of the Apostles, who worked with Christ's direct authority. The benefits of the salvation Christ won for us by his death and resurrection were imparted to children by grace – not because they deserved it or had made a personal decision, but by grace – and that was in accord with the Gospel. Later, children might repudiate their place within the New Covenant; but for the time being they unquestionably belonged.

The Old Testament pattern

It is the same with priesthood. Consider the New Testament alone, and it is hard to make a convincing case for a set-apart priesthood; bishops and deacons, yes – but about priests we really cannot be sure. Consider the whole Bible, however, and the cultural setting it created for the early Church, and the case is overwhelming. The offering of sacrifices, and the receiving and offering of the gifts of the people, was a task done in Old Testament times only by the priests in the line of Aaron. They alone could bless in God's name and perform the ritual acts that made the people clean for God's service. Other trained leaders, like the Rabbis, might teach the faith, instruct the young and look after the affairs of the local synagogue. But only the priests performed those special acts that formed the worship of the Temple. Inevitably this God-given pattern would colour the practice of the early Church. It ought to have done, for God clearly intended it to do so! It was a God-given pattern, and was there to guide and give form to the Church as it emerged from its Jewish roots.

Clement, Bishop of Rome, writing about AD 96, clearly regards the orderliness of the Jewish pattern of worship as a model that binds the Church. It does not even occur to him to equate Christian ministers with the Jewish priests; but he insists that only those divinely authorized to do so should celebrate the Christian Eucharist, just as only the Old Testament priests could offer the Temple sacrifices:

> All these things are plain to us who have scanned the depths of sacred lore. It follows, then, that there ought to be strict order and method in our performance of such acts as the Master has prescribed for certain times and seasons. Now, it was his command that the offering of gifts and the conduct of public services should not be haphazard or irregular, but should take place at fixed times and hours. Moreover, in the exercise of his supreme will he has himself declared in what place and by what persons he desires this to be done, if it is all to be devoutly performed in accordance with his wishes and acceptably to his will. Consequently, they who present their offerings at such appointed time are accepted and blessed, since the care with which they observe the Master's laws clears them of all offence. The High Priest, for example, has his own proper services assigned to him, the priesthood has its own station, there are particular ministries laid down for the Levites, and the layman is bound by regulations affecting the laity.
>
> In the same way, my brothers, when we offer our own Eucharist to God, each one of us should keep to his own degree. His conscience must be clear, he must not infringe the rules prescribed for his ministering, and he is to bear himself with reverence. The continual daily sacrifices, peace-offerings, sin-offerings and trespass-offerings are by no means offered in every place, brothers, but at the altar in front of the Temple; and then only after a careful scrutiny of the offering by the High Priest and the other ministers aforesaid. Anything done otherwise than in conformity with God's will is punishable with death. Take note from this, my brothers, that since we ourselves have been given so much fuller knowledge, the peril that we incur is correspondingly graver. (Clement of Rome, *Letter to the Corinthians* 40–41)

At first Church practice may well have been what we might call irregular. 'They broke bread in their homes and ate together with glad and sincere hearts' (Acts 2:46). We have an impression of the Lord's Supper being celebrated in every home in the setting of ordinary family meals. But before long they came to realize that they could not so casually celebrate the Holy Eucharist (1 Cor 11:17–33); for in doing so they were offering before God the eternal sacrifice on the cross of his Son. In bringing to his Table their alms and their offerings of bread and wine they were presenting before him themselves, to be cleansed and refreshed for his service. These were priestly acts that should be done in Christ's name by those who were called and set apart for the purpose.

A clearly defined ministry

When the Apostles set up a Church in a new place they chose suitable men from among their first converts and ordained them as authorized leaders for the community (Acts 14:23). Sometimes a leader was called an elder (*presbyter*), sometimes an overseer (*bishop*); the terms were used interchangeably (Titus 1:6–7). These men appointed assistants (deacons) to share in the worship and evangelism of the Church and to take charge of its administrative and charitable work (just as the Apostles had done in Acts 6). It was a clearly structured pattern intended to regulate the worship and life of the Church. St Paul, writing to the Philippians, addresses his letter 'To all the saints in Christ Jesus at Philippi, together with the overseers (bishops) and deacons' (Phil 1:1). We note that 'bishops' (or elders) are in the plural. Bishop Clement of Rome regarded this as the normal pattern.

> When the Apostles had been given their instructions, and all their doubts had been set at rest by the resurrection of our Lord Jesus Christ from the dead, they set out in the full assurance of the Holy Spirit to proclaim the coming of God's kingdom. And as they went through the territories and townships preaching, they appointed their first converts – after testing them by the Spirit – to be bishops and deacons for the believers of the future. (Clement of Rome, *Letter to the Corinthians* 42)

Very soon, however, this first structure had to be sharpened up in order to counter the heresies that started troubling the Church. In the large cities like Antioch, Christianity was encountering the mystery religions of the Near East; people from many backgrounds started flocking into the Church, bringing with them their former beliefs, which they then tried to graft onto the Christian teaching they received. One error was to suppose that the Son of God had not really walked this earth in a body of flesh; he had only appeared to do so. He was not born as we are, they said, and did not die as we do; his sufferings were only an illusion (the heresy known as *docetism*). This was an error that arose even in the time of the Apostles (see 1 John 4:2–3 and 2 John 7). It turned the story of

Jesus into little more than a myth, and the Eucharist into a meditation using Christian symbols. It threatened to submerge the Church in the mish-mash of cults that teemed in that part of the world.

The error had to be resisted; but how? At that stage there was no accepted body of New Testament Scripture to turn to; and the heresy had infected even the body of presbyters (or bishops). There were a few Apostles still left, but they were ageing and not readily available. The Church dealt with the problem by according to the leading presbyter the duty of deciding which other presbyters and their congregations were true to Christ, and which not. Henceforth only this leading presbyter was called the bishop, and he alone was seen as the fountainhead of ordination and authority in the Church. Bishop Ignatius of Antioch seems to have taken the lead in this development; but it quickly caught on across the Christian world, and by the time Bishop Ignatius came to write a set of letters to other Churches in Asia Minor (about AD 106) they all had highly respected bishops whose role was accepted in the manner Ignatius approved.

> Abjure all factions, for they are the beginning of evils. Follow your bishop, every one of you, as obediently as Jesus Christ followed the Father. Obey your clergy too, as you would the Apostles; give your deacons the same reverence that you would to a command from God. Make sure that no step affecting the Church is ever taken by anyone without the bishop's sanction. The sole Eucharist you should consider valid is one that is celebrated by the bishop himself, or by some person authorized by him. Where the bishop is to be seen there let all his people be; just as wherever Jesus Christ is present, we have the world-wide Church. Nor is it permissible to conduct baptisms or love-feasts without the bishop. On the other hand, whatever does have his sanction can be sure of God's approval too. This is the way to make certain of the soundness and validity of anything you do. (Ignatius, *Letter to the Smyrnaeans* 8)

This separating of the functions of bishop and presbyter seems to have occurred across most of the Christian world before AD 100, quite possibly many years before – we do not know just when. But Ignatius became Bishop of Antioch about AD 69, when several of the Apostles were still active. When he wrote his letters, the new role of the bishop was a well-accepted institution. One of these letters was to the Church at Ephesus, whose bishop Onesimus he met; by well-attested tradition the Apostle John lived out his days at Ephesus. He must have been aware of the new development; and we may assume his tacit approval.

Protestants need to realize just how good this evidence is. We may not in the New Testament find bishops leading colleges of presbyters, as we now have it; but we do find bishops (equally known as presbyters) leading every New Testament Church that we know about. The development happened when there were Apostles still around, and must have earned their approval. Just as infant baptism did not need apostolic approval, so the single bishop in charge of a diocese was so natural and necessary a development that it needed no special authorization. The Holy Spirit was just quietly leading the Church forward, and nobody ever doubted it – until the Reformation.

In the early years the Church could not use the word 'priest' (except of the Lord Jesus Christ); it would have confused its Jewish members impossibly. Those authorized to preside at the Eucharist had no connection with the priests of the tribe of Aaron in the Jewish system. However they were performing what everyone recognized as a priestly function; and by the end of the second century the word 'priest' was slipping naturally into the Christian vocabulary. Eventually it came to be the only word used of the second order of ministry – until the Reformation.

Holy to the Lord

The Jews had a very strong concept of holiness. Originally, the term was used of things set apart for God's service. The vessels employed for offering the gifts and sacrifices were holy – set apart for God's service, and not to be used for other purposes. The priests who conducted the worship were also set apart, holy; the garments they wore were holy, and to be used only for the Temple worship; and the diadem on the High Priest's turban bore the inscription: HOLY TO THE LORD (Exod 39:30). Places where God had revealed himself in special ways were perceived as holy; when Jacob awoke from his famous dream he says: 'Surely the LORD is in this place, and I was not aware of it! . . . This is none other than the house of God; this is the gate of heaven' (Gen 28:16–17). And he set the place apart for himself and his family, and gave it the name 'Bethel', which means 'House of God'. When Moses met God at the burning bush, he was told that the place where he was standing was 'holy ground' (Exod 3:5), and he must behave appropriately. The day set apart for rest and worship, the Sabbath, was 'holy' (Exod 31:15) – along with other special times and seasons.

Things set apart for God's service – holy things – were to be suitable for the service of a God who was above all else himself holy. The Temple and everything in it was to be specially and beautifully made. Holy days were not to be profaned with unsuitable activity. Above all, the people involved were to seek a moral purity like that of God himself: 'Therefore be holy, because I am holy' (Lev 11:45). It was therefore appropriate that the early Church decided to set apart some people for the central act in its life of celebrating the Lord's Supper, the Holy Communion, and would come to see these people as priests of the New Covenant.

It was not only appropriate but intended by God that this should happen; why else would he have moulded the Jewish culture into this form? He had chosen and shaped it as the culture within which his Son should be revealed and the early Church emerge. Undoubtedly the Apostles he had chosen for the task guided and approved this developing pattern of Church order. There is no doubt at all that the early Church leaders in the post-apostolic period saw an order of priesthood as an essential part of the tradition they had received and must pass on. Protestants can ignore such evidence only by denying all authority to the writings of the early Church Fathers. At the least these writings form commentaries on the Scriptures, which carry vastly greater weight than the works of protestant theologians from another culture many centuries later.

It was also necessary for everyone to know that those who undertook the work of a priest were not self-selected, but appointed and commissioned by the central authority of the Apostles; and there is plenty of New Testament evidence that this is exactly what the Apostles arranged. It was necessary that the Eucharist should be seen as an act of the whole Church, not as something that a particular group of believers decided to do on their own initiative.

Gifts shared out

In setting apart some as priests, the early Church was not denying the priesthood of all believers; for this too was well-known Old Testament teaching: 'Although the whole earth is mine, you will be for me a kingdom of priests and a holy nation' (Exod 19:6). This is the passage alluded to in the First Epistle of Peter where the New Testament people of God are described as 'a chosen people, a royal priesthood, a holy nation' (1 Peter 2:9). There was nothing inconsistent with setting apart some as priests, in order that the priesthood of the whole people should be realized. The priesthood exercised by the priests was none other than the priesthood of Christ himself, bequeathed to the Church for the whole human race until its fulfilment in the final kingdom of God. The Catechism puts it like this:

Christ, high priest and unique mediator, has made of the Church 'a kingdom, priests for his God and Father'. The whole community of believers is, as such, priestly. The faithful exercise their baptismal priesthood through their participation, each according to his own vocation, in Christ's mission as priest, prophet and king. Through the sacraments of Baptism and Confirmation the faithful are 'consecrated to be . . . a holy priesthood'.

The ministerial or hierarchical priesthood of bishops and priests, and the common priesthood of all the faithful participate, 'each in its own proper way, in the one priesthood of Christ'. While being 'ordered one to another', they differ essentially. In what sense? While the common priesthood of the faithful is exercised by the unfolding of baptismal grace – a life of faith, hope and charity, a life according to the Spirit, the ministerial priesthood is at the service of the common priesthood. It is directed at the unfolding of the baptismal grace of all Christians. The ministerial priesthood is a *means* by which Christ unceasingly builds up and leads his Church. For this reason it is transmitted by its own sacrament, the sacrament of Holy Orders. (CCC 1546–1547)

Our Lord Jesus Christ shares his priesthood with the whole body of believers, but never the whole of it with one person. Rather he apportions it between us, so that the whole body acting together should do his work in the world. We do not expect all believers equally to express every aspect of Christ's priesthood. Some are called to one part of his work and some to another. The role of the priest, set apart within the company of believers, is one of enabling the ministry of the whole company, and of helping build it up through word and sacrament for its God-given task.

It was he who gave some to be apostles, some to be prophets, some to be evangelists, and some to be pastors and teachers, to prepare God's people for works of service, so that the body of Christ may be built up, until we all reach unity in the faith and in the knowledge of the Son of God and become mature, attaining to the whole measure of the fullness of Christ. (Eph 4:11–13)

The gifts of each are meant to support the ministry of all, and only the whole Church acting together can expect to express fully the all-embracing priesthood of Christ: 'You are the body of Christ, and each one of you is a part of it' (1 Cor 12:27).

There is a simple spiritual principle operating here. All things may be set apart as holy to the Lord; indeed all things should be. But unless some things are especially set apart, in practice none will be. You may worship God anywhere; but unless some places are set apart for that purpose, there will be little worship anywhere. You may pray and worship God any day of the week, but unless one day is set apart for this, it will scarcely happen at all. The priesthood of all believers is an ancient and scriptural doctrine. But unless some believers are set apart for the priestly ministry, there will be little real priestly work at all. It is a God-given pattern, written deeply into Scripture and the nature of human life; and we are foolish to attempt to deny it.

6: A CHRIST-LIKE MINISTRY

Must the Church have bishops, priests and deacons? Catholics say 'Yes, undoubtedly'. Many protestants say 'Perhaps, but we can manage without'. So let us ask a slightly different question: Does a true Church contain within its ministry *episcopacy* (the ministry of bishops), *priesthood* (the ministry of priests), and *diakonia* (the ministry of deacons)? The answer must be a definite 'Yes'.

A true Church must have ways of encouraging and correcting its life and witness, so that it continues true to Christ and in unity with the rest of the Church. That is *episcopacy*, or Christ-like oversight.

A true Church represents God before the world, and the world before God. Before the world it proclaims the saving work of Christ, before God the sacrifice of Christ on our behalf. So it imparts the life and saving power of Christ by word and sacrament, and bears its witness to him and draws others to know him. That is *priesthood*, or Christ-like ministry.

A true Church cares and serves with all the self-denying, self-effacing love of Christ, and so makes the presence of Christ credible to an unbelieving world. That is *diakonia*, or Christ-like service.

I cannot prove from the Bible that the three orders of ministry – bishops, priests and deacons – are a necessary feature of the Church, though if we bring in the evidence of the early Church Fathers that is the inevitable conclusion. We cannot prove from the Bible that the Apostles simply passed on their ministry to bishops; nor may we really identify the presbyters of the New Testament with the later priests, or Stephen and his companions of Acts chapter 6 with the later deacons (let alone the probationer priests of our day). But there is no doubt that the three-fold ministry of Christ is to be found wherever he is loved, worshipped and obeyed. From the earliest times we find the Church exercising oversight of its congregations; to start with mostly by the Apostles, but before long delegated to others like Timothy and Titus. In the Church at Pentecost we see much priestly ministry and diakonia, initially in the hands of the Apostles, but very soon shared with others – and to some extent with the whole Church. We can confidently assert that the Church has always exercised the three-fold ministry of Christ. If Christ dwells in the Church, its true life and work can only be an extension of his life and work as we see it in the Gospels; and always a Christ-like ministry is a unifying ministry that draws people together and resists division.

Early in the second century the pattern of ministry became explicit by the establishment of the three orders of ministry – bishops, priests and deacons – though at that stage priests were referred to as *presbyters*. The effective witness of the Church was enhanced by this, just as it was strengthened as the list of books that made up the New Testament gradually came to be accepted. These were not new things set up by the Church as an administrative afterthought. The first need was for an authentic ministry to pass on to a needy world the new life and the new lifestyle given by Christ. Alongside this was the need for authentic teaching, guaranteed true to Christ by those who should know. At first both functions were exercised by the Apostles. But local leaders arose, commissioned by the Apostles to direct the life and mission of the local Church; amongst these the more experienced, with a more than local reputation, sought to keep the local Church in step with the worldwide Christian community and corrected deviations of teaching; they there-fore were the ones who alone could commission new local leaders. Alongside this was the work of service in the local community, which the new life in Christ required; again this was initially led by the Apostles, but was soon passed to others. Priests, bishops, deacons – an inevitable pattern in the life of the Church.

The authentic Gospel

Always there was the need to assert the historical foundations of the Church. They were able to say: This ministry derives from Christ and his Apostles, and has his authority. This bishop received it from another bishop who received it from the Apostles of Christ himself. This priest and that deacon are accepted by the bishop as true ministers of Christ. The Gospel we proclaim to you is authentically that given by God through Christ his Son, and the new life we minister to you by word and sacrament is authentically that given by Christ through his Spirit. The continuing historical ministry of bishops, priests and deacons is the guar-antee of the authenticity of the word and sacrament ministered.

The Gospel would be passed on through individuals commissioned for the task; and they would have at their elbows the authentic documents that came down from those earliest moments of the Church's life. Errors were bound to creep in. But the sharing together of the worldwide leaders would protect against the worst follies. And the Spirit of the living Christ at work among them would ensure that the forces of evil would not ultimately prevail. Such a Church, with such a Gospel, was bound to take the form it did – around bishops, priests, and deacons, doing the work and ministry of the Apostles and teaching from the apostolic documents – with the Holy Spirit to guide them.

Many protestant denominations claim to have jettisoned the historic orders of the Church: but have they? They have certainly not jettisoned the *functions* of bishop, priest and deacon. They claim to have no one set apart as a priest; but they are very careful whom they allow to celebrate the Holy Communion. Those so chosen are carefully trained to it, and are required to be adept at interpreting the Scriptures. Such people are the ones who in practice decide what is scriptural, and what is not. They claim to have no bishops; but their leaders are relied on to distinguish the true from the false, and by their communications with one another to authenticate congregations and individuals. They are insistent in claiming continuity with the earliest times, not only through the Scriptures, but also through the successions of faithful congregations by which their own Church came into being. They have not really given up the idea of having bishops, priests and deacons; but by not being in communion with the rest of the Church they have raised doubts about those who exercise these functions among them. Are these people really bishops, priests and deacons, and are the sacraments they minister and the word they preach really those of Christ? Are these people really the true Church, or not? And it is left to personal judgement to decide.

But Christ and his Apostles did not leave this to be a matter of personal judgement. We all bear personal responsibility for our choices; but selecting which is the true Church is not one of them! For there is only one, and wilfully to join something else is to leave Christ's Church. Agonized protestants will exclaim: 'Yes, that is all very well. But what do you do if the *true* Church has departed from the *truth*?' The answer must always be: Play your part in bringing it back to the truth; but never separate. You have the Scriptures and the Spirit of Christ as your allies, and the Lord will not in fact allow the true Church ultimately to go wrong. If, through the actions of your forefathers you find yourself separated, then come back as soon as you can do so with integrity. Praise the Lord if you have come to faith in your time of separation; praise him for all you have learnt of him and for his promises on which you have rested your soul; praise him if perhaps you have been called to his service, and have been used by him to make known his love and bring others to faith. But come home as soon as you can. And if your obligations to others compel you for the time being to stay apart, make sure it is only for a short time.

Anglican orders

The Anglican Church is almost alone among the reformed Churches in claiming to continue the faith and order of the Church in unbroken succession through the time of the break with Rome in the sixteenth century. Other reformed Churches made a complete break with tradition, and went back to the Scriptures to fashion a new faith and order on that basis; their ministry and forms of Church government were thought out afresh, as well as the credal statements to which they subscribed. But the Church of England retained the creeds and the decisions of the early Church Councils, and continued with the ministry of bishops, priests and deacons inherited from the medieval Church.

The one change it made was to deny the supreme authority of the Pope. Instead, the English Sovereign in parliament took the right to make the ultimate decisions. Parliament took the place of the Pope. The first aim of Henry VIII and Elizabeth I was to leave everything else unchanged. In the event they were forced to change a great deal, partly to accommodate the more radical protestant thinking of many in the Church, but chiefly in order to make the break with Rome effective; there must be nothing left that would draw the people back to the old religion with its Roman traditions and associations. But the ministry of the Church they kept: bishops, priests and deacons, would continue as before, presided over by the archbishops of Canterbury and York, as set up in the time of Augustine. It appealed to the *English* sense of tradition, while excluding the *Roman* tradition. The Church of England has always insisted that its orders are those of the Catholic Church; it emphasizes that its bishops and priests are ordained, not into the Church of England, but as bishops and priests of the Church of God.

The question arises whether a Church whose ministers function apart from the Catholic Church can still claim to have the same orders of ministry. Historically they can point to their catholic origin; but can Anglican bishops genuinely claim to be bishops of the universal Church, when they owe no allegiance to it and are not in communion with it? If they deny the role of the Pope as the focus and source of unity in the Catholic Church, can they really claim to be catholic bishops at all? If the bishops who ordain are not catholic bishops, neither are the priests they make catholic priests, nor are their sacraments catholic sacraments. They are serving a different and non-catholic religion.

The Church of England was set up to be both *catholic* and *protestant: catholic* in preserving the inherited pattern of ministry, but *protesting* at the Church being controlled from Rome. Anglo-catholics in the Church of England resent being called protestants. But, if they are refusing the authority of the universal Church, protestant is the correct term to describe their position. You do not become catholic by adopting a particular style of worship and beliefs; you are catholic by being a member of the universal Church. Beliefs and styles of worship follow from that. We can all be grateful to the anglo-catholics for keeping alive in England these ancient Church practices with their great wealth of spirituality; but they were always protestants and will remain so until they rejoin the Catholic Church. Valid orders are not a matter of pedigree, but of the body to which you belong. In a Faith with historical roots, origin and pedigree of orders are important. But their present validity depends on present obedience within the order of the universal Church.

As long as the protest of the Church of England was against the way things were done from Rome, its position was just logical. The Church of England could claim to be the 'ancient Church of this land, catholic and reformed' (*The Revised Catechism*, 1962). It could claim to be the true heir of Augustine and of the first Christians in England. It would remain part of the universal Church set up by Christ, even if the rest of Christendom fell away. It was not ashamed to admit its need of reform, and waited patiently for the rest of the Church to catch up. Then, of course, it would re-unite.

But the Lord has now called that bluff. The rest of the Church has 'caught up', and do they still mean to stay separate? What are they protesting at now? The protestant spirit is a spirit of independence that wants to go its own way; and this is what now rules in the Church of England. The claim to be both catholic and protestant is a contradiction in terms. To be catholic is to be united with the universal Church; and to be protestant is to be separate and independent. You cannot be both things at once.

The classic Anglican position was summed up in what was called the Lambeth Quadrilateral, set down by the Lambeth Conference of Anglican bishops in 1884 and re-affirmed in 1920. They listed four elements whose 'whole-hearted acceptance' should be the basis of a new unity between the Churches. These were (i) the Holy Scriptures, (ii) the historic Creeds, (iii) the sacraments of Baptism and Holy Communion, (iv) an episcopally based 'ministry acknowledged by every part of the Church'. But this minimum position has now been grievously eroded; for the Anglican Church has in recent years been changing the inherited pattern of its ministry, with the result that it is no longer acknowledged by many even of its own members, let alone by the rest of the Christian world.

This is not the only respect in which parts of the Anglican Communion are embracing a liberal Christian agenda; and they are doing this, not in order to reform for scriptural or other doctrinal reasons, but in order to respond to the pressure of current Anglo-Saxon thinking. The rest of the Christian world may never see this as the way of truth; and so the Anglican Communion may have set out on a path that permanently diverges from everyone else. The Anglican claim to be still *catholic* depends now on the rest of the Church one day deciding to follow the Anglican way. We shall see. History will tell. But whatever happens, the Anglican Church seems to want to be free to decide its own future in its own Anglo-Saxon way; and it is doubtful whether it will ever want to do otherwise. This is not a *catholic* way of thinking.

The matter is complicated by the presence in the Anglican Church of many Christians who are out-and-out protestants and deny the validity of priestly orders altogether. This, the evangelical party, is happy to have bishops and priests as a *useful* means of running the Church and maintaining its discipline; but they do not see them as a *necessary* part of the Church's being. If the developing needs of the Church required it, they would be happy to see bishops and priests abolished – through the usual constitutional processes of the Church of England. For them this would not in any way affect the essential nature of the Church as the body of Christ. They acknowledge the usefulness of the bishop as the focus of unity in a diocese. They allow him a role in leadership, but they do not *need* bishops in their religion. They like a bishop to preach the truth, but they do not see him as the guardian of the Faith once delivered to the saints; that is a role they reserve for the Bible alone. The presence in the Anglican Church of a substantial party who do not believe in bishops or priests must cast further doubt on the Anglican claim to have the same orders and sacraments as the universal Church.

For all these reasons the Catholic Church denies the validity of Anglican orders and sacraments, while acknowledging their catholic origin. For them Anglican orders and sacraments are defective in their *intention*. Anglicans, they say, intend to do something different from the Catholic Church in these things. Even if some Anglicans (the anglo-catholics) mean to do the same, they intend to go on doing so in separation; and that is not a catholic intention. Anglicans are producing bishops and priests of a different Christian religion with similar but different sacraments, and catholics cannot pretend there is no difference. Actually Anglicans intend a whole range of different things in their orders and sacraments. The official Anglican stance is that these varying intentions are parallel and valid understandings. The Catholic Church cannot accept this; for some of these Anglican positions are quite contradictory to received teaching, and a complete denial of the sacramental nature of the Church.

Until recently there has been an assumption on the Anglican side that one day the two Churches would reunite. The ecumenical movement of the twentieth century and the ARCIC discussions between Anglicans and Catholics made this seem more and more likely. Both Churches, they said, would grow, develop and reform, under the guiding hand of the same Holy Spirit. He would lead us eventually to grow together in truth, to the point at which we could in total honesty recognize each other's orders and sacraments; and people would then hardly notice the change. But that was Anglican thinking, expressed again very fully by David Edwards in *What is Catholicism?* He cannot see why Rome should not wish to proceed steadily along that path. But Rome remains cautious, seeing all too clearly the radical difference between the two Christian religions, catholic and protestant, and knowing full well the ability of Anglican protestantism to re-assert its desire for independence. This it seems now to have done in an irrevocable way.

Completing the Reformation

The sixteenth-century Reformation came at the end of a long period of preparation, in which ideas and possibilities slowly grew and developed in people's minds. The change when it came was sudden and decisive. The schism was the work of human beings, but God was insisting on *reformation*. If the Church refused to reform, it was bound to split. God cannot allow his Church to continue in error. Protestantism developed a spirit of independence and wanted to go its own way; this was no part of God's purpose. But insofar as the protest was against error, God could and did use it to renew his Church.

Now, I believe, God is insisting on unity, and it is the turn of protestants to change. All through this century we have enjoyed a lively period of growing together in all the Churches, with deepening respect and understanding. It has been a long period of preparation. Now once more we are approaching the moment of decision. The hallmarks of the true Church, and therefore of its ministry, are listed in the Nicene Creed: it must be One, Holy, Catholic and Apostolic. The Reformers insisted on a *Holy* ministry which was to be truly *Apostolic* (which, amongst other things, implied a *scriptural* ministry). Our generation is coming to see that the Church and its ministry must be *One*, and we begin to suspect that the only way of doing this is for the Church, and its ministry, to be *Catholic*. We cannot indefinitely continue with two separate Christian religions. The hand of God was certainly there in all the turmoil of the Reformation; and he did not desert his Church in its separation. But I doubt whether he will let it continue separate much longer.

Anglicans, and protestants generally, do not realize that the Catholic Church has already for its part turned the corner of radical change. It may be some time before the teachings and attitudes of the Second Vatican Council are absorbed at all levels in the Church; but already it has fully embraced the great positive teachings of the Reformation. It presents protestants with a serious challenge. The Lord has taught protestants much during their time of separation; and all of this is ready to be shared with the whole Church. He has also preserved among protestants the ideal of a Christ-like ministry, and the Anglican Church has preserved even its form. It is time for protestants to give up their ideas of independence. For a truly Christ-like ministry must unite the Church, not divide it. The Second Vatican Council opened the door to new relationships between the Catholic Church and other Christians. Now is the time for protestants to return to the fold in which they really belong.

7: THE NONCONFORMIST EXPERIENCE

The arguments we have deployed for a ministerial priesthood uniting the whole Church are unlikely to weigh much with nonconformists, for their experience contradicts the whole idea. Many evangelicals in the Church of England are nonconformist at heart, and will also feel uneasy, shaking their heads and saying: 'There must be something wrong with such reasoning.'

We must admit with shame that historically nonconformist experience of bishops and priests has been a very negative one. They have seen bishops who lorded it over their people, and priests who used their positions as a power base to swell their egos and their pockets – men in cassocks who manipulated their communities and peddled superstitions to enthral men's minds. It is not a pretty story, even if amongst the charlatans there were some real saints, humble redeemed sinners whom everyone respected and who did a great job for their Lord. No wonder many nonconformists have come out from the mainstream Church, saying: 'We will have nothing to do with it; we hate the whole system, sacraments, priestly orders and all!'

Indeed, loyalty to Christ may well have put them in an intolerable position. We dare not judge them for their action; for the fault lay mostly with the mainstream Church. It was the same when the Church of England parted from Rome in the sixteenth century: there were intolerable errors and corruptions in the Church throughout Europe; also Henry VIII wanted unfettered control of Church life in England. And so the separation came.

Reunion obligatory

The first call of every Christian is to follow Christ. Loyalty to the truth may bring us into conflict with other Christians if there is serious error in the Church. Such tension may be more than we can bear, and lead to breakdown of fellowship. Our Lord does not desert us in such an exile, whoever is at fault; but his leading will always be towards renewal and eventual restored unity.

It is a fundamental protestant error to suppose that we are free to pick and choose the church we shall attend. We see people move house and then look around for the church that takes their fancy. Obedience to Christ cannot be expressed that way: he demands a stability of commitment, in which personal taste and preference do not enter at all. Nothing should ever be allowed to disrupt this mutual acceptance and belonging. However, gross error in the Church will always be a threat to its unity; for it must set those who are loyal to Christ in opposition to those who are drifting into error.

There is a theology to be heard in parts of the House Church movement: it claims that God has rejected the mainstream Churches, and is calling out a new Church to be ready for the Lord's return. This cannot be sustained from Scripture. God never rejects the people he has chosen. 'God's gifts and his call are irrevocable' (Rom 11:29). Again and again we see God judging his people, in order to bring them to repentance and renewal; but he never rejects. He has not cast off his ancient people, the Jews; for they are bound to him in a most solemn covenant, in which it is impossible for God to deny himself.

Likewise he will not reject the Church he founded on the Apostles, though he may need often to judge it and renew it. 'The gates of Hades will not overcome it', says our Lord (Matt 16:18). You may be sure that the forces of evil will do their worst, aided at every step by human wilfulness and sin. But the Lord knows very well how to keep his Church and preserve it in the truth. There may be much lifeless clutter in the mainstream Church and much that should be judged. But if our Redeemer does not know how to renew the Church he first set up, then the House Churches had better look to their own fellowships, for he does not know how to renew them either – and it will be necessary before long, we may be sure!

There can be no conceivable programme for Church development that does not include eventual organic reunion. 'Unity in diversity' is a slogan that has captured the imagination of our generation of Christians, but like most slogans it is only a half-truth. For without organic union there is no unity. With organic union there is plenty of scope for cultural diversity; without it cultural diversity becomes cultural divergence, until those involved no longer feel they belong to the same body. See how it is with the Church of England and the Methodists. They have been apart barely 200 years, but already the cultural divide between them is so hard to bridge! A mere four and a half centuries separates all the other Churches from the Roman Catholics, but to many in England the Catholic Church seems like another world. The growing together of the Churches in the last forty years has made some of these divisions seem much less – to the point where some Christians can float happily from one Church to another. But for Christians with a strong commitment, changing Churches is still a radical thing to do.

If we claim to be obedient to Christ, there can be no other Church programme than eventual reunion – Methodists, Anglicans and the rest, united once more with Rome. She is the Mother Church of the West. We cannot plan for anything else. Protestants are fond of saying they could only rejoin Rome if Rome changed. But Rome *has* changed, and protestants never noticed! Rome is as much *reformed* now as the protestant Churches – in many ways more so. It is not hard to point out doctrinal differences. But if the Catholic Church in the sixteenth century had been what it is now, there would have been no real reason to separate. Vigorous internal debate would have produced all the adjustment that was necessary.

Grace and faith

Catholic laity are now encouraged to read the Bible and think about it for themselves, and some at least do so more faithfully than many protestants. The doctrine of *justification by faith* divided the Churches radically at the Reformation; for protestants it was the cornerstone of their theology, and gave them grounds for refuting much of the teaching they heard from Rome. But all this has changed – much of it in the last thirty years, though actually there was a long period of preparation before that. Here are some extracts from the recently published Catechism of the Catholic Church to warm the hearts of protestants:

The first work of the grace of the Holy Spirit is *conversion*, effecting justification in accordance with Jesus' proclamation at the beginning of the Gospel: 'Repent, for the kingdom of heaven is at hand.' Moved by grace, man turns towards God and away from sin, thus accepting forgiveness and righteousness from on high. . . .

Justification *detaches man from sin* which contradicts the love of God, and purifies his heart of sin. Justification follows upon God's merciful initiative of offering forgiveness. It reconciles man with God. It frees from the enslavement to sin, and it heals.

Justification is at the same time *the acceptance of God's righteousness* through faith in Jesus Christ. . . .

Justification has been *merited for us by the Passion of Christ* who offered himself on the cross as a living victim, holy and pleasing to God, and whose blood has become the instrument of atonement for the sins of all men. . . .

Justification establishes *co-operation between God's grace and man's freedom*. On man's part it is expressed by the assent of faith to the Word of God, which invites him to conversion, and in the co-operation of charity with the prompting of the Holy Spirit who precedes and preserves his assent:

'When God touches man's heart through the illumination of the Holy Spirit, man himself is not inactive while receiving that inspiration, since he could reject it; and yet, without God's grace, he cannot by his own free will move himself toward justice in God's sight.'

Justification is the *most excellent work of God's love* made manifest in Christ Jesus and granted by the Holy Spirit. It is the opinion of St Augustine that 'the justification of the wicked is a greater work than the creation of heaven and earth', because 'heaven and earth will pass away but the salvation and justification of the elect . . . will not pass away'. . . .

Our justification comes from the grace of God. Grace is *favour*, the *free and undeserved help* that God gives us to respond to his call to become children of God, adoptive sons, partakers of the divine nature and of eternal life.

Grace is a *participation in the life of God*. It introduces us into the intimacy of Trinitarian life: by Baptism the Christian participates in the grace of Christ, the Head of his Body. As an 'adopted son' he can henceforth call God 'Father', in union with the only Son. He receives the life of the Spirit who breathes charity into him and who forms the Church.

This vocation to eternal life is *supernatural*. It depends entirely on God's gratuitous initiative, for he alone can reveal and give himself. It surpasses the power of human intellect and will, as that of every other creature. (CCC 1989–1998)

The jargon is not entirely what protestants are used to; but it is all so different from the hard-line sayings we used to hear. It may be a long time before the whole Church has caught up with these insights. There are bound to be lingering elements (on both sides) of older nineteenth-century ways of thinking; but the old barriers have crumbled, and can never be rebuilt. Many people, however, are still fearful of crossing the ground they were built on.

So why do we stay apart now? The reason lies, of course, in the cultural divergence between us. The Catholic Church seems to many protestants like a foreign land. But cultural divergence is a purely human thing, a thing responsible moreover for most of the divisions and negative thinking in our world. Our Lord fortunately understands about purely human things, for he became one of us, and lived his life surrounded by some of the most rigid cultural barriers the world has ever known. Yes, he understands. But ultimately he knows, as we do deep in our hearts, that there is only one place for purely human things like this, namely at the foot of his cross – to be buried with him, so as to find new life in him. The Gospel has no problem with cultural *diversity*, which our God apparently rejoices to see filling every corner of his world. But it is another matter when cultural *divergence* has driven a wedge between the parts of his Church – which he created to be united in its witness to the world. His separated children have an obligation to come together. It will be as painful as crucifixion, but that is where grace is to be found.

Positive sacramental experience

Many nonconformist *ministers* – who do not claim to be *priests* – have been greatly used by God to bring the grace of Christ effectively to their flocks and to the world around. Almost all of them use faithfully the sacraments of baptism and the Lord's Supper, as well as other sacramental ministries like the anointing with oil for healing; and they find in these acts the grace and saving power of Christ.

As a young man I once attended some Bible studies organized by a group of the Christian Brethren – a denomination that is deeply committed to the weekly celebration of the Eucharist. We were studying the First Letter to the Corinthians, and came in due course to chapter 11, where St Paul gives some basic teaching about the Holy Communion. At first the younger people in the group spoke up and presented one form of the classic evangelical teaching on the subject: that the Eucharist is just an act of remembrance, putting us in mind of all that the Lord did for us on the cross – *and nothing more*. But after a pause an older man said: 'Yes, I know I was taught that when I was young; but I have not found it so. It is far more than a memorial act. I have met the Lord in the Breaking of Bread in a way that I cannot compare with anything else in my Christian experience.' Then one by one the older folk in the group spoke up and talked of their experience of the real presence of Christ in the Eucharist using language that would have done credit to any catholic.

There was no denying the powerful collective experience of that group of Brethren; and it will all be echoed by many other faithful nonconformist Christians. They know they have experienced in full measure by word and sacrament the grace and love of our Lord Jesus Christ and the power of his Spirit. 'So', they answer us, 'why do we need priests? We have one priest, the Lord Jesus Christ himself, the only mediator between God and mankind; and we need no other. It is through his grace alone that we have experienced his living touch in the sacraments.' A catholic dare not deny this testimony, for it is through the grace of Christ alone that he too meets with his Lord at the Eucharist. This encounter with Christ is not a privilege accorded only to the right party in the Church. It is by his grace alone that we all live.

But . . . how can we be *sure* where and when we will meet with the Lord? For though the grace of Christ is available to all, it is not there at our beck and call to be turned on like a tap when we are in the mood. It is given at times and in manners of his sovereign choosing, and our choice is only whether to receive or to reject.

'Lord, can I wait till tomorrow?'

'Why wait, my child? I have chosen *this* moment for you. It is the *best* moment – and it is the *only* moment. I shall love you still tomorrow, but *this* opportunity will have passed.'

His dealings with us are infinitely loving; but there is severity in his mercy, for this is what we need – not only at our first turning to the Lord, but at every stage of our Christian lives. God is not playing games with us. 'I tell you, *now* is the time of God's favour, *now* is the day of salvation' (2 Cor 6:2). All who are serious about following and obeying our Lord Jesus Christ will be given opportunities to find his grace; the Lord will see to it in his own way and at his own time. Thank God there are so many nonconformists who have found and embraced the grace of Christ in the sacraments. But how can we or they be *sure* of meeting him in their sacraments *always*, when these are conducted outside the fellowship and discipline of the universal Church? That is the problem to be faced.

Sacramental assurance

The ways God uses to touch our lives are infinitely various; indeed we live in a sacramental universe – in which anything may become the vehicle of his loving touch. But there are ways he has set apart, and made holy with his presence – in which he promises to be present always. These are the *Holy Scriptures* and the *Holy Sacraments* given to the Church by our Lord, in particular *Holy Baptism* and *Holy Communion*. Here there are no ifs or buts; he *promises* to be present. He does not say 'If you are good, I will meet you at the Holy Communion'. No! He *is* there, always. He does not say 'If you really believe (whatever that means), I will meet you in the waters of baptism'. He *is* there, with all his saving power; and we may have total confidence in that.

So with the Bible: it is the word of God, and he speaks to us through it. We may come to it with darkened minds and unwilling hearts, and fail to heed the message. But he speaks through it all the same. And we may come to the sacraments casually and without recognizing his presence. He is there just the same, but his presence then brings only judgement on our souls. 'For anyone who eats and drinks without recognising the body of the Lord eats and drinks judgment on himself. That is why many among you are weak and sick, and a number of you have fallen asleep' (1 Cor 11:29–30). The judgement of the Lord is not contrary to his love; rather it is just the severe side of it, and can even be the means of bringing us to repentance.

He means us to be quite certain about these holy things, in which he promises to meet with us. With the Bible, there must be no doubt about what writings go to make it up; and here there is a residual problem between catholics and protestants about the Apocrypha – and it ought to be cleared up, very quickly; for it is based on dubious assumptions made by our forefathers. With baptism, it must be perfectly clear what exactly Christian baptism amounts to, and whether a particular person has received it. And when Christians meet together to break bread, it needs to be clear beyond any shadow of doubt whether this is the sacrament of the body and blood of Christ. For it is an action of the universal Church, the timeless action of the Eucharist, carried out in fellowship *with angels and archangels and all the company of heaven*. This is why we need priests, commissioned for the task by the universal Church in a universal order deriving from Christ and his Apostles.

With nonconformist ministers and their flocks we cannot be *sure*. They have chosen to be separate and do their own thing. Perhaps Christ in his love and mercy meets them on at least some occasions – perhaps on every occasion; but how can we be certain? We see much evidence that he has met with many of them in the past, for their lives and their testimony show it. But we cannot know when and where it will happen again. Brothers and sisters, if your ministers were priests in the universal Church we *would* know – and, I think, so would you.

THE ROCK FROM WHICH WE WERE HEWN
The challenge of authority

I am weak in the discharge of my office and lacking in application; when I want to act with dedication and energy, I am held back by the frailty of my very nature. This may be so. But our Priest, almighty and eternal, is unceasing in mercy towards us; one like us and yet equal to the Father, he has brought his divinity down even to the human, and raised humanity to the divine. The source of my joy, as is right, is the plan which he made: for in giving the care of his sheep to many shepherds, he himself did not relinquish the custody of his beloved flock.

Pope St Leo the Great, fifth century, *Sermon 3 de Nativitate* 2–3

8: DIVINE AUTHORITY

The Church has always been troubled by problems of authority, and probably always will be, human nature being what it is! When authority tries to push us around, we resist and query its right to do so. In human affairs this must be a wholesome reaction; authority may be able for a time to coerce, but in the end its right to rule comes only from our consent. But with God it is different; for his authority does not depend on our consent. He gives us freedom to accept it or reject it, but either way his authority remains absolute, for it rests on truth. There is no tyranny in God's authority, and we know he seeks only our good; but all of us start by trying to avoid it. For divine authority exercised in a sinful world is bound to be uncomfortable; it must challenge our ways. We may know in our consciences that here is the voice of God, and yet our first reaction will certainly be to resist.

This is the verdict: Light has come into the world, but men loved darkness instead of light because their deeds were evil. Everyone who does evil hates the light, and will not come into the light for fear that his deeds will be exposed. (John 3:19–20)

God does not usually confront us with a direct display of his presence and power, which would virtually take away our freedom to choose. He makes his authority known indirectly, perhaps through the Bible or a Christian minister. The problem then is to recognize the teaching we hear as from God.

Those who met our Lord in the Gospels faced this difficulty. He knew that he came with the authority of the Father, but how were they to know that? Those who ruled the Temple in Jerusalem challenged him: '"By what authority are you doing these things?" they asked. "And who gave you this authority?"' (Matt 21:23). Jesus answered by challenging them with the same question about the authority of John the Baptist: '"John's baptism – where did it come from? Was it from heaven, or from men?"' (Matt 21:25). And they refused to answer; for, unlike many of the common people, the chief priests and elders had not accepted John's teaching as from God. If they had, their hearts would have been prepared to recognize Jesus. John had preached repentance in terms they could understand; but they had not repented, and so their hearts were closed against further dealings with God. There was a fundamental untruth in their lives; and they would understand no more of God until it was removed. (If they had stayed around, they would have heard John actually point to Jesus as the Messiah, the Saviour who was to come.)

The principle God uses in asserting his authority on earth appears to be this: he approaches us first through things we understand; if we respond, our hearts will be prepared to go further, and we are then able to see his authority behind the messenger he sends. The Jews who confronted Jesus said they trusted the teachings of Moses. But Jesus tells them their trust could only be skin-deep, or they would believe in him as the one Moses wrote about:

> If you believed Moses, you would believe me, for he wrote about me. But since you do not believe what he wrote, how are you going to believe what I say? (John 5:46–47)

In a formal way they accepted the Scriptures and attended to them. But they had not allowed the Scriptures to *dwell* in them.

> The Father who sent me has himself testified concerning me. You have never heard his voice nor seen his form, nor does his word dwell in you, for you do not believe the one he sent. You diligently study the Scriptures because you think that by them you possess eternal life. These are the Scriptures that testify about me, yet you refuse to come to me to have life. (John 5:37–40)

Only when we have responded to the light we have, through Scripture and through other teaching that probes our consciences, only then will we see clearly who really speaks for God in this world. Christians who have problems with authority need to look closely at their consciences to see if they are resisting the Lord.

The servants of the Lord

In the last analysis we have to assess God's servants through their works – 'you will know them by their fruits' (Matt 7:16); and our Lord submitted himself to the same test: 'The very work that the Father has given me to finish, and which I am doing, testifies that the Father has sent me' (John 5:36).

The final seal on our Lord's work was of course his resurrection. But during his earthly ministry all who met him had to make a provisional assessment on the basis of what they saw and heard. He never wanted people to be too impressed with the miraculous and the charismatic, both of which were present in his work; in any case miracles never convince those whose hearts are set against him. 'The miracles I do in my Father's name speak for me, but you do not believe, because you are not my sheep' (John 10:25–26). The assessment he wanted them to make was on the *goodness* of his work. Did it glorify God? Could they see his Father working through him? And only those whose hearts were prepared by repentance, and by allowing his word to *dwell* in their hearts, could see it.

The authority of the servants of the Lord is to be assessed in the same way. Is their work *good?* Does it glorify God? Can we see God at work through them? Sometimes at least the people of God will answer with a joyful 'Yes!' Sometimes they will sadly shake their heads. Mostly, if the Spirit of Christ is moving freely in their hearts, they will rejoice where they can see the Lord's hand in the life of his servant; and where it is otherwise they will turn lovingly to prayer – for they will believe that the same loving Redeemer is at work in the life of his servant as in themselves. Love has no problem with authority, as long as the people can see that the good Lord is at work among them.

The cross and the glory

The world at large will not be so charitable. The failings of a priest they will pick on gleefully – we see it often in the newspapers. But in so doing they are at least acknowledging the divine standard by which everyone is judged. If it is wrong for the priest it is wrong for everyone else too. They are scandalized when a priest goes off the rails, but at least this shows they know the difference between right and wrong – for the priest and for themselves – and are condemning themselves also.

Where however the life and witness of a priest stir their consciences uncomfortably, they will either be angry, or try and ignore him; and their irritation is then not against him, but against the Lord who so potently works through him, and troubles them. Again the priest represents the authority of the Lord, and they know it and resent it.

The minister of the Gospel must expect the same treatment his Lord received – to some extent crucifixion, which he must accept for Christ's sake. But also he will experience a love that he does not begin to deserve. For there will be many for whom he has been a channel of grace; and as they respond to the Lord they bestow on his servant a love that is out of all proportion to his worth in himself. This too he must accept humbly for Christ's sake.

There is no room in the priest for anything but humility, as he offers himself to be the Lord's channel of grace for his people. To find himself used by the Lord is a wonder; and often God uses him *in spite of himself.* The Church he represents is a strange creation of God's love; it is almost ridiculous how God uses weak and fallible human beings to shed abroad his love among us, and to make known to a needy world the truth as it is in Jesus. But this is the way he has chosen. He honours and exalts the whole human race by giving his Church so great a responsibility – and the authority with which to carry it out. He trusts us to use that authority wisely in his name.

9: ON THIS ROCK

The Lord Jesus Christ has always retained immediate control over his Church. The earliest creed was the statement 'Jesus is Lord' (1 Cor 12:3). By that they did not mean he was the distant figurehead of the Church, the emblem on its banner. Nor did they mean he had given them rules to follow, and left them to work it all out as best they might. He set up a structured Church with leaders commissioned to carry forward his work; but he never handed over control to those leaders. When they said 'Jesus is Lord' they recognized his direct and immediate control over the affairs of the Church. As he left them at the Ascension, he promised paradoxically to be 'with them always' (Matt 28:20); and the Holy Spirit was sent to make his immediate presence effective and to guide the Church 'into all truth' (John 16:13).

Our Lord looks for our co-operation. When he receives it, we have the joy of knowing that he is working through us, and we can all see his authority expressed in his Church. When we fail to go his way and are unresponsive to his leading, he is not outwitted; God is never mocked.

But authority then becomes a burden hard to bear, and the whole Church is in travail, until once more Christ rules in our lives at all levels. Much of Church history has been occupied with such hard labour; and so it is not surprising that many have rejected the authority structure of the Church as an unacceptable imposition.

However, it is the structure set up by the Lord Jesus. In the Gospels we see it only in embryonic form, and in the rest of the New Testament only in its first developments towards the mature pattern. But by slow degrees it grew from there into the fully-fledged organization that emerged onto the historical stage. David Edwards in *What is Catholicism?* sets out very fully the historical process by which the government of the Church reached its eventual form. It is mostly a sorry tale of human weakness and muddle, and through much of the Middle Ages, of downright wickedness. If we are examining the historical record for confirmation of the authority of the Church we shall search in vain. All we see is a power struggle, often ruthlessly pursued, and carried out by the most worldly methods. In no way can the Christian conscience find here the proof of divine authority; and David Edwards is right to emphasize the point. We look in vain for the seal of divine approval in the record of either the Catholic or the Protestant Church. Both may point to their saints, who prove much about the grace of God; but neither should attempt to veil its failings, which show only the depth of human sin from which we need redeeming.

But because things went wrong, more than once, in all sorts of ways, this does not justify us in rejecting the Lord's chosen structure pattern for his Church. Our task is to take warning from past failures, and to seek to rebuild the structure and use it, as he intended. So we need to enquire exactly what the structure was that the Lord set up, and look carefully how it started to develop under the hand of his Apostles.

The Lord's structure

The Lord Jesus set up a pattern of concentric circles. The most obvious was that of the Twelve; they were called to leave their secular employment and be constantly with him. They were to see the way he did things and be witnesses of his teaching and actions. Within that circle was an inner group – Peter, James and John – who alone witnessed certain very confidential moments, such as the raising of Jairus' daughter, the prayer at Gethsemane, and the great vision of the Transfiguration. There was also a circle of women who travelled with Jesus, and helped support the party in practical ways (Luke 8:1–3); some of these were to be the first witnesses of the resurrection (Luke 23:55 and 24:9–10).

Outside the Twelve were other circles, sent on particular missions, such as the 72 in Luke 10; and beyond them the whole body of disciples: 120 in Jerusalem on the eve of Pentecost, and 500 who saw the Lord after his resurrection on a mountain in Galilee. Peter was to be leader and spokesman of the Apostles, and therefore of the whole body.

The responsibility for passing on the revelation the Lord saw as a *shared* task. Only he himself possessed the full light of the Spirit. The Twelve would share that light, and had *collective* responsibility in finding the way forward. The understanding given to one needed to be corrected and balanced by the light given to the rest. When the Lord sent out mission parties, always he sent them two by two; the need for mutual support and correction is a universal principle, followed normally by the early Church. St Peter, called by special divine guidance to go to the Gentiles in the house of Cornelius, takes along with him 'some of the brothers from Joppa' (Acts 10:23).

Even so the other Apostles and the rest of the Church in Jerusalem do not automatically accept Peter's *irregular* action (as it seemed to them at first). He is called to task (Acts 11:1–3), and has to relate exactly what happened, so that they can all see God's hand in it and agree that it accords with the Lord's word in the Gospels. Only then do they accept Peter's action as valid.

On at least one occasion Peter was demonstrably in the wrong on a fundamental issue (Gal 2:11), and had to be rebuked and corrected by Paul – a rebuke which, as far as we can see, he accepted humbly. No one regarded him as infallible. The Apostles individually had no special protection from failure. As though to make the point Peter, their leader, denied the Lord, and had to be specially restored; and Judas Iscariot betrayed him, and never came back. The Church has always known that its chief pastors have no special protection from error and failure. Dante, writing in the Middle Ages, has a Pope or two sizzling in the nether regions of his *Inferno;* and perhaps surprisingly for protestants, Dante got away with it!

What is the rock?
The Petrine text in Matthew 16 has been more bitterly fought over than any other passage in the Bible: libraries of books have been written about it, so I am foolish even to quote it. And here is a matter on which I must take issue with David Edwards; for in *What is Catholicism?* he queries the prominent use of this text in the Catechism of the Catholic Church, and therefore in any Christian apologetics. His argument is that here we have a statement that critical scholarship shows as probably

not from the lips of Jesus. The parallel passages in Mark and Luke report only a much simpler statement from Peter: 'You are the Christ' (Mark 8:29 and Luke 9:20), and do not include Jesus' answer, naming Peter as the Rock on which he would build his Church. Also the word 'church' is not one that Jesus (or any other contemporary Rabbi) would have used; it seems to be imported from later Church usage. The implication is that the passage carries a much reduced authority if it is not really a word from the lips of Jesus. This implication I reject utterly, both as a catholic and as an evangelical. Whatever the route by which this passage arrived in our text, it is still part of the authoritative word of God; and the Church is obliged to treat it as such. It may well be true that these words of Jesus were inserted later by St Matthew or by the Church in Alexandria that finally edited and published the Gospel. But that does not detract from their authority.

Rightly understood, this result of critical scholarship carries another meaning that evangelicals are not used to considering (or catholics for that matter). It is an important meaning, central to the argument of this book.

If these words were put into the mouth of Jesus by the later editor of the Gospel, then evidently, even in the apostolic period, the Church felt free to report as words of Jesus teaching which it had received later from the Holy Spirit. It made no difference whether the words were actually spoken by Jesus, or were received from him through his Spirit. They were all part of the revelation of the eternal God brought to us in Christ. Of course this way of thinking opened the door to every charlatan who wanted to peddle false teaching; and the Apocryphal New Testament (the set of early documents the Church never accepted as Scripture) shows how extensive this literature was. Even in the apostolic period the only protection against this was the true Tradition of the Church, as lived out in its congregations and mediated by the authentic teaching Magisterium of the Church. These three things, Scripture, Tradition, Magisterium, belong together as a closely integrated medium for revealing the truth as it is in Jesus. As the new Catechism puts it (quoting from the Second Vatican Council document *Dei Verbum*, 1965):

It is clear therefore that, in the supremely wise arrangement of God, Sacred Tradition, Sacred Scripture and the Magisterium of the Church are so connected and associated that one of them cannot stand without the others. Working together, each in its own way, under the action of the one Holy Spirit, they all contribute effectively to the salvation of souls. (CCC 95)

So now – with, I hope, renewed confidence – let us turn to what the word of God requires us to believe about the Church and Peter.

'But what about you?' Jesus asked. 'Who do you say I am?'

Simon Peter answered, 'You are the Christ, the Son of the living God.'

Jesus replied, 'Blessed are you, Simon son of Jonah, for this was not revealed to you by man, but by my Father in heaven. And I tell you that you are Peter, and on this rock I will build my church, and the gates of Hades will not overcome it. I will give you the keys of the kingdom of heaven; whatever you bind on earth will be bound in heaven, and whatever you loose on earth will be loosed in heaven.' (Matt 16:15–19)

Protestants have argued that the word 'rock' referred to the faith in Christ expressed by Peter's words; or else that it referred just to a *fragment* of the underlying *bedrock* on which houses might be built. Christ is the *bedrock*, they say, Peter just a *fragment*. But the Greek word *petra* (rock) is just the ordinary word for rock, and cannot carry such subtle meanings. Besides, there is the obvious play on words with Peter's name – *Petros* in Greek. Protestants will do anything rather than accept that the 'rock' in our Lord's statement is Peter – which is the natural meaning of what he said. Catholics have too easily accepted his words without noticing why Peter's answer made him suitable in our Lord's eyes to be the rock on which he could build his Church. The dust of conflict has made the position of each side invisible to the other!

Yes, Peter was the rock on which our Lord proposed to build his Church; and there is no escaping this clear meaning of the Petrine text. But it was a Peter who had just spoken a truth about Jesus that had been directly revealed to him by the Father. He had not puzzled it out in his own mind; he had not debated it with the others and taken a vote on it. It was a direct inspiration of the Holy Spirit from the Father, and Peter had allowed himself to be God's spokesman. In making Peter the rock on which he would build his Church, our Lord was also accepting him as the spokesman of the truth into which the Church would be guided by the Holy Spirit; the two things go together. We build the Church when we speak the truth about Jesus in the power of the Holy Spirit; and it is then built into the structure founded on Peter.

Our Lord had plans for only one Church, and that would be the one founded on Peter. Peter was a fallible human being and made mistakes. His mistakes did nothing to help the Church – except perhaps to underline vividly the difference between Peter the Lord's spokesman, and Peter the weak human being. Matthew wants us to be quite clear about this, for in the continuation of the story he has Peter trying to deflect Jesus from his passion and crucifixion, which earned him the stinging rebuke: 'Get behind me, Satan! You are a stumbling block to me; for you are setting your mind not on divine things, but on human things' (Matt 16:23). The Apostle Peter was to be the foundation on which the Church would be built; he was also quite capable of being a stumbling block to the Lord and to his fellow disciples. It is a strange and paradoxical situation, and we have to come to terms with it. The Lord was going to build a Church which the forces of evil would not be able to overcome. Errors of doctrine, false practices, and unholiness of life, would all creep into the Church from time to time, but would not overcome it. Overall the Church would be true to its Lord in doctrine and practice, and would be a genuine fount of holiness.

Only a Saviour who is completely confident of his capacity to defeat the forces of evil could contemplate building an infallible Church on very fallible human beings. But then we have such a Saviour. When we say we believe in the Church, it is an expression of faith in the *Saviour* of the Church; for it is only his presence within it that makes it reliable.

This is the Church as we know it – even in the local parish. Here is a priest, who is anything but infallible, but used as a channel of God's grace. What matters is what God accomplishes through him. It is the same at every level: bishops, archbishops, patriarchs and Popes – to say nothing of all the lay people – fallible and limited human beings every one of them, but used by our Lord to form the ongoing structure of the Church in which he dwells, and which he protects and controls. And it was all founded on an Apostle who was no better than any of them; what God accomplished through Peter was to build an enduring monument to the grace and power of our Lord Jesus Christ. We listen to the Church because Jesus speaks through it, and for no other reason.

Speaking for God

If Peter is a fallible human being, how can we know for certain when he speaks for God? In his statement before the Lord Jesus: 'You are the Christ, the Son of the living God' (Matt 16:16), we know he spoke truly because Jesus says so. But at other times, must we just exercise private judgement as best we may? The answer lies in the structure the Lord set up to carry forward his authority in the Church. The college of Apostles bore a collective responsibility. When they supported their leader and spokesman then the Church would know that Peter was speaking for

God. The prototype occasion was the day of Pentecost: 'Then Peter stood up with the Eleven, raised his voice and addressed the crowd . . .' (Acts 2:14). At that point the twelve Apostles enshrined in themselves the teaching and tradition bequeathed by Jesus, which would in due course be preserved in the New Testament documents and in the life of the Church. Peter standing with the other Apostles spoke the truth from God, and spoke infallibly. The Holy Spirit honoured and confirmed that word in the response he called forth from the people. As long as we confine our thinking to Christ, Peter, the Apostles, and the New Testament record, protestants have no problem. The difficulties arise when we talk about the Pope as the heir of Peter, and the bishops as the heirs of the Apostles, and the Pope as their infallible spokesman.

Let us deal with Apostles first. Even in the New Testament the word 'Apostle' is used ambiguously, for it did not refer only to the Twelve. The Twelve were all Apostles, set apart as the unique witnesses to Jesus and his teaching; and when they needed to fill the gap in their number created by Judas Iscariot, they looked for someone who was a witness to the resurrection and had been with them throughout the ministry of Jesus (Acts 1:21–26). There were only a few who qualified, and they chose Matthias. It is clear that the supply of suitable witnesses was very limited, and the Twelve could never be replaced when they died.

But the word 'Apostle' was applied to others, who were not among the Twelve – Paul and Barnabas, for instance (Acts 14:14). Paul in his letters writes as an Apostle (e.g. Rom 1:1), and he often had to defend his Apostleship against those who doubted it. The early Church was quite used to the idea of Apostles other than the Twelve, for we find it protecting itself against 'false Apostles, deceitful workmen, masquerading as Apostles of Christ' (2 Cor 11:13); and the Church at Ephesus is congratulated because they 'have tested those who claim to be Apostles but are not, and have found them false' (Rev 2:2). The word 'Apostle' simply means 'one sent out'; and we get the impression that the early Church had many such people circulating among its communities, some properly authorized, and some not. These latter were just peddling their own ideas. But the ones who came with the apostolic authority of the Twelve were true guardians and teachers of the Gospel.

When the Twelve had all died, the Church still needed *guardians* of the Faith, to speak with *apostolic* authority and be the focus of its unity; and this is what the bishops are. Individual bishops may go off the rails, but collectively they define the truth, just as the college of Apostles had done.

The early Church went further than this, recognizing that the Lord had chosen an inner circle of leadership (in Peter, James and John). This was how the Church saw the bishops of those Churches which were original apostolic foundations, such as Antioch, Alexandria, Rome, and so on. These Churches were the custodians of treasured memories (and probably documents) of the original apostolic ministry. Their bishops held a special responsibility in preserving the unity in truth of the universal Church. They were the inner apostolic circle, and came eventually to be called *patriarchs*.

The bishop of Rome

It would be lovely and straightforward if we could say that the Church then went on to reckon the bishop of Rome as chief of the patriarchs, the successor of Peter in the structure pattern the Lord had set up. But rivalry and inter-regional disputes prevented this from happening. The bishop of Rome was indeed often asked to adjudicate in Church disputes. Decisions on doctrine or Church practice were seen as requiring the agreement of the bishop of Rome; and no Council of the Church could have universal authority without the involvement of the bishop of Rome. The Council of Constantinople in 381 (which, however, had no representative from Rome) recognized the primacy of the bishop of Rome, on the basis of Rome being the first city of the Empire. But this fell short of acknowledging the Roman Church's own claim to primacy on the basis of its joint foundation by Peter and Paul.

From the Gospel record we must conclude that the Lord means there to be someone to act as the focus of the Church's unity. He does not allow room for parts of the Church to claim the guidance of the Holy Spirit, and then do as they see fit, regardless of the rest. In the Gospels the Lord set up a clear structure pattern, with a particular human being as the focus of unity. Peter was designated as the leader and spokesman of the apostolic band. When he articulated their common mind he spoke with all the authority of Christ. This is how the Catholic Church sees the role of the Pope among his bishops.

The Lord made Simon alone, whom he named Peter, the 'rock' of his Church. He gave him the keys of his Church, and instituted him shepherd of the whole flock. 'The office of binding and loosing which was given to Peter was also assigned to the college of Apostles united to its head.' This pastoral office of Peter and the other apostles belongs to the Church's very foundation and is continued by the bishops under the primacy of the Pope. (CCC 881)

There can be only one focus of unity. Ideally the bishops agree, as the Twelve did at Pentecost; and Peter then speaks for them. But in the real world they will not always agree; and then the Church needs a successor of Peter, someone accepted as the central focus of unity. Disagreement can continue (up to a point!), but the true bishops of the Church are those who accept the successor of Peter; and the true Church is that which accepts the true bishops. It is not just a nice theory. It is the way the Lord means it to be; it is his chosen structure pattern, clearly set out in Scripture.

The trouble was that the Church of the fourth century could not agree on how to handle its internal government. Frequently the problems of the Church were resolved only by the intervention of the State. Even the selecting of its bishops often needed the strong arm of the State to settle party rivalries. It is amazing that in this situation the Church succeeded in settling many of its deep doctrinal problems in a way that has stood the test of time. The Great Councils of the fourth and fifth centuries eventually reached a common mind in these matters, which all the main streams of Christianity have fully accepted. But on Church government they were less successful. The involvement of the State in Church affairs never seems to be a recipe for peace and stability – as the record of the English Church miserably confirms.

However, the twentieth-century Church is at last free to escape from this, and has the freedom to act on its own spiritual judgement, without reference to any State. So our generation can look again at the Lord's intended structure pattern for his Church. He has seen to it that there is still only one possible successor of Peter, namely the Pope, the bishop of Rome. All that is lacking is our acceptance of him. When the heir of Peter speaks God's truth with the backing of the heirs of the Apostles, and the Holy Spirit calls forth a response from the whole people of God, then we should listen. For the Lord himself is addressing us.

10: HOW DOCTRINE DEVELOPS

We do not need to understand much Christian doctrine in order to receive the salvation brought to us by our Lord Jesus Christ. Very few who encountered Christ in the Gospels had any idea who he really was; but he captured their hearts and won their allegiance and they became his followers – and so they found the salvation he offered. When Jesus saw Matthew sitting in his tax booth and said to him 'Follow me', we do not know what passed through Matthew's mind. But he 'got up and followed him' (Matt 9:9). After that everything was different for Matthew. An eternal transaction had occurred between him and Almighty God, and slowly, slowly he would come to understand it and learn how to explain it to others.

It is the same with all of us. The challenge of Christ comes to us, to each in a different way; and we respond. The mind is involved, but what matters is the response of heart and will. It is enough to know that Jesus is the Saviour of the world, and of me in particular, and then to step out trustingly in obedience. Understanding comes later – and will never be complete, however long we live. God deals with us all differently; and there may be some (though I have yet to meet one) whom God approaches through the intellect; but even then his purpose is to win their love and allegiance. Undoubtedly his preferred way for all of us is that we should be brought up in a Christian home, surrounded by prayer and affection, and hearing from our earliest years the stories of Jesus from those who trust him and follow him; even before we can build conscious memories he wants us to share in our families and in the Church the experience of prayer and worship. He would like us all to emerge from childhood already in a growing relationship with the Saviour. Many people, baptized and brought up as Christians, do just that; a proper understanding of the Gospel comes only later as they mature.

Understanding is important, but secondary. It is vital for all of us that *head knowledge* should not get too far ahead of *heart knowledge*. What matters in Christian doctrine is what affects life; and we never really understand a doctrine until our behaviour is controlled by it. Without that practical outcome we are just playing intellectual games, and God is not interested in that. Ideally, understanding and obedient response go hand in hand. We cannot understand the truth about our God without the help of the Holy Spirit; and he only works in our minds if our lives are yielded to Christ. Then mind and heart are in step together; doctrine controls behaviour; and we are learning how to live. This is the path of true discipleship.

Doctrine in the Church

It is significant that St Paul always started his letters with doctrinal exposition; then he would draw out the practical conclusions that followed. Most of his letters were to correct some abuse or error in the Church; and he begins with doctrine. For instance the first eleven chapters of the Letter to the Romans are given over to a profound exposition of the Gospel. Then at the beginning of chapter 12 there is a monumental 'therefore', followed by three chapters of instruction on Christian behaviour. He saw that the way the Church behaves depends on the doctrine it believes. Wrong behaviour flows from doctrine poorly understood. So when he saw something amiss in the Church it drove him to dig more deeply into the doctrine of Christ. Get the doctrine right, at least with those whose hearts are obedient to Christ, and the rest would follow.

This is the way God works, both with us as individuals and with the Church as a whole. Life presents us with challenges and puts us on the spot. Then by prayer and with the aid of the Scriptures and the wholesome tradition of the Church, and with such wise advice as we can muster, we explore what God is leading us into. So we come to understand him better, as we find the way forward. Discerning the right path can be an unnerving process full of uncertainty, but God is in it, working creatively in our lives and in the whole Church, so that generation by generation the Church knows him better and the world sees him more clearly.

Our Lord, who taught his disciples so much during his short time with them, knew that there were some things he should not reveal at that stage, because they were not ready for them: 'I have much more to say to you, more than you can now bear. But when he, the Spirit of truth, comes, he will guide you into all truth' (John 16:12–13). The point at which we can 'bear' a new truth is the moment when we need it to guide our actions. Then, if we follow the guidance given (and only if we do), we come to understand the doctrine. Life calls forth practical wisdom, and understanding follows: this is God's way with the whole Church. In every generation the Church confronts new situations, and is guided to apply afresh the truths it knows; so it gains a deeper understanding of the doctrines it has inherited and sees them in a clearer light.

The Apostles had collective authority in guiding the Church of their time, like the bishops in later periods. But Apostles and bishops can only pass on to the Church the truths it is ready to receive and able to 'bear'. This is the method of the Lord, and Apostles and bishops are committed to following the way of Christ in all things. All down the ages, truths emerge in the Church as they are needed, and there is every reason to think this will go on until the Lord returns. The Apostles, with their unique experience, probably understood far more than ever appeared in their letters. They knew, as Jesus did, that they had more to give, but they also knew that the Holy Spirit would be at work in the Church after their departure and was well able to continue guiding it into all truth. There is nothing in the New Testament to suggest that the revelation of truth ceased with the death of the last Apostle. (The warnings and anathema in Rev 22:18–19 refer only to the Book of Revelation and not to the whole New Testament, which had not at that stage been collected together.)

Doctrine grows and develops as the Church needs it. In one sense it is all there in the New Testament; but only in the way that an embryo holds all the parts of the full-grown adult. The protestant position, that all the truth we need is to be found in the Bible, is only partly right. Yes, it is all there in the Bible; but it needs the pressures and strains of developing Church life down the centuries to call forth the hidden truth so that we may see and believe.

> 'The Christian economy, therefore, since it is the new and definitive Covenant, will never pass away; and no new public revelation is to be expected before the glorious manifestation of our Lord Jesus Christ.' Yet even if Revelation is already complete, it has not been made completely explicit; it remains for Christian faith gradually to grasp its full significance over the course of the centuries. (CCC 66)

For instance the doctrine of the Holy Trinity is all there in the Bible, but it is not so immediately obvious that the first Christians could not debate the matter endlessly. Only by stumbling down several false trails, and after many generations of sometimes unseemly argument, would the Church eventually arrive at a clear understanding of it.

Protestants accept the doctrine of the Trinity, and receive the Creeds in which it was enshrined; but they then turn their backs on the historical process the Holy Spirit used to get the Church there. The same historical process was also guiding the Church forward in other areas of doctrine. Here protestants have difficulties, for the doctrines in question – about the Church and about Mary for instance – belong in a system they dislike and distrust. In this section we have tried to present the doctrine of the Church in a new light; later we shall look more closely at the doctrines about Mary, an area in which protestant distrust is particularly acute.

But let us be fair and admit that the Holy Spirit was also at work behind the traumatic events of the Reformation period that bred this protestant distrust, and that he has used it in guiding the Church and keeping it from losing its way down yet another false trail. Let us go on from there and allow that the hand of our God has brought us to the point now where we can look on this mysterious historical process with a measure of enlightenment, and even with humour. Protestants, do you accept the providence of our God in history, quietly moving the human story forward towards God's intended destiny, and gently protecting his Church so that it continues to be the channel for his grace and love in the world? If so, you should accept the Catholic Church as his, as well as believing that *you* have a part to play in his purposes.

A growing organism

The picture that emerges, of the Church and of the pattern of doctrine
it enshrines, is of a growing plant. The life and whole potential of the
plant is contained in the rootstock and first shoots set up in the soil of
the world. It is all there at the beginning, but only gradually do we see
what form the plant will take as new shoots sprout and develop into
branches. No two branches are quite the same, although all follow the
same basic principles of growth; but what those principles are only
becomes apparent as the mature tree develops. Each branch is constantly adapting to circumstances; one has to grow around obstacles;
another needs more light and air; yet another is smotheringly tangled
with the undergrowth. In each branch the inner life-force of the plant
reacts appropriately, and no one can tell what form the growth will take
until it happens. Observing it, we might for a time disagree about the
principles at work, but eventually it will become clear to us what is really going on. If the original plant contained within itself the resources to
respond rightly to every eventuality, then the final result will be as
intended.

The body of doctrine the Church lives by will grow and develop, as
life calls forth the new insights that are needed. Doctrine always develops; for the Church's perception of itself and of the world around it, and
therefore its understanding of its God, is constantly changing. This
principle applies just as much to the protestant Churches as to the
Catholic Church. Protestants may say their doctrine is unchanging,
being founded on Scripture; but the fact is that the pattern of doctrine
accepted in the Church of England (or the Methodist Church or any
other) is not the same as it was 200 years ago, or even fifty years ago.
Doctrine develops; in a living Church nothing can prevent it. Some
basic things may seem unchanging, like the doctrine of the Trinity. But
even this will be seen differently as time progresses and the Christian
culture perceives it in new ways.

In the sixteenth century protestants came to think that much of the
growth of the Church from the early centuries had been false. So they
separated. Cut off from the main plant, they endeavoured to graft themselves back into the early rootstock of Christ and his Apostles and the
Scriptures. But to re-enter that moment in Church history would have
required really a return to the culture and personalities of the first century; and they were in the sixteenth century. There was no way of going
back and creating a new shoot of the old first-century tree. In reality
they became a separate plant, relating indeed to Christ and the Scriptures, and therefore bearing much of the truth, but lacking the God-

given developments of the Church in the early centuries, through which it had received much of its doctrine and structure.

A role for tradition

Protestants are familiar with the principle that one part of Scripture must not be interpreted so as to contradict another. But if perception of doctrine is a developing thing in the Church, then the unfolding tradition of the Church must also stand alongside the Scriptures, and the one be used to throw light on the other. Just as tradition may not conflict with Scripture, so Scripture is to be understood in the light of tradition.

In keeping with the Lord's command, the Gospel was handed on in two ways: – *orally* 'by the Apostles who handed on, by the spoken word of their preaching, by the example they gave, by the institutions they established, what they themselves had received – whether from the lips of Christ, from his way of life and his works, or whether they had learned it at the prompting of the Holy Spirit'; – *in writing* 'by those Apostles and other men associated with the Apostles who, under the inspiration of the same Holy Spirit, committed the message of salvation to writing'. . . .

This living transmission, accomplished in the Holy Spirit, is called Tradition, since it is distinct from Sacred Scripture, though closely connected to it. Through Tradition, 'the Church, in her doctrine, life and worship, perpetuates and transmits to every generation all that she herself is, all that she believes'. . . .

'Sacred Tradition and Sacred Scripture, then, are bound closely together, and communicate one with the other. For both of them, flowing out from the same divine well-spring, come together in some fashion to form one thing, and move towards the same goal.' Each of them makes present and fruitful in the Church the mystery of Christ, who promised to remain with his own 'always, to the close of the age'. . . .

As a result the Church, to whom the transmission and interpretation of Revelation is entrusted, 'does not derive her certainty about all revealed truths from the holy Scriptures alone. Both Scripture and Tradition must be accepted and honoured with equal sentiments of devotion and reverence.' (CCC 76–82)

This is well understood in the Catholic Church. The great Church Councils never contradict earlier Councils; Popes do not nullify the pronouncements of their predecessors. For to do so would cast doubt on the whole developing pattern of Church doctrine, and therefore on their own teaching. The teaching authority of the Church depends on maintaining the authority of the whole tradition, including the Bible.

The task of giving an authentic interpretation of the Word of God, whether in its written form or in the form of Tradition, has been entrusted to the living teaching office of the Church alone. Its authority in this matter is exercised in the name of Jesus Christ. . . .
  'Yet this Magisterium is not superior to the Word of God, but is its servant. It teaches only what has been handed on to it. At the divine command and with the help of the Holy Spirit, it listens to this devotedly, guards it with dedication and expounds it faithfully. All that it proposes for belief as being divinely revealed is drawn from this single deposit of faith.' (CCC 85–86)

Protestant Churches also have a developing tradition; but by definition this carries almost no authority, since for them authority rests in Scripture, not in tradition. What the Church has *traditionally* taught is neither here nor there; for any protestant is free to disagree with the teaching, and many constantly do. Some protestants now foolishly question even the scriptural basis of the Church's doctrine, and everything then becomes a matter of personal opinion. The ultimate folly is seen when questions of truth are decided by a democratic vote. Why should a majority of sinful human beings be right? But for all the absence of effective teaching authority in the protestant Churches, the Holy Spirit still touches protestant hearts, and uses faithful protestant Christians to witness to the love of Christ. We have a God who is more gracious than many catholics have yet discovered!
  At first sight the catholic insistence on Tradition looks likely to make the whole system fossilize hopelessly. But in practice it does not work like that. Earlier teaching is never rejected, and doctrines do not change; but they are perceived differently. The Second Vatican Council never contradicted either the sixteenth-century Council of Trent or the nineteenth-century First Vatican Council, and never needed to; but its perception of the nature of the Church was radically different, and has led the Church forward on a path that seemed unthinkable thirty years ago. Not least was its recognition of a place in God's purposes for the protestant Churches. Progressive protestants now find the Catholic Church open to the future in a breathtaking way. Evangelicals see the Catholic Church consulting the Scriptures (along with the Fathers who first received them) in a way not often heard in protestant Church

Synods; for the Bible and the Fathers are part of the tradition, and may not be laid aside without sacrificing the whole authority of the Church. The Catholic Church cannot jettison its *catholicity*, its continuity from the beginning; for that is its guarantee of divine protection.

Ultimate truth in Christ alone

Our Lord's promise of the Holy Spirit to 'guide into all truth' applies to the Church down the ages, not just to the Twelve who heard it. The Holy Spirit has not been withdrawn; and always, if the Church is listening and obedient, he guides it. The trouble is that the Church is not always listening and obedient; and so it stumbles, as the congregations did to which St Paul wrote his Letters. Then the Church has to learn its doctrine afresh and return to truer ways. The Church thus seems to follow a halting and erratic path, stumbling and picking itself up, losing its way – and then, apparently by accident, on course again.

The progress of the Church through history does not inspire confidence in the outside observer. But then the world is not supposed to place its faith in the Church, but in the Lord who guides it. The world may look with amusement and scorn at these holy fools who make up the Church. But then it may also notice with amazement that the eternal God appears to be in partnership with them, and is revealing his love in them. Somehow he keeps them from falling flat on their faces, and in a world full of upheaval and change these 'ridiculous' Christians still obstinately stand for the truth and still smilingly point to the ultimate meaning of life to be found in the Lord Jesus Christ. The Church is a crazy organization; but this does not matter a bit, as long as through the Church the world gets a glimpse of our wonderful God.

One point on which the Church has always been perfectly clear and explicit is that the whole truth is to be found in Christ, and in him alone. Christ embodies the truth in a unique, special and complete way; and through him alone may humanity come to the Father from whom all truth derives. Christ is the truth and the wisdom at the heart of all things; he is the one through whom this universe was created and through whom it is held in existence.

> He is before all things, and in him all things hold together. . . . For God was pleased to have all his fulness dwell in him, . . . in whom are hidden all the treasures of wisdom and knowledge. (Col 1:17, 19; 2:3)

> I am the way and the truth and the life. No-one comes to the Father except through me. (John 14:6)

All things have been committed to me by my Father. No one knows the Son except the Father, and no one knows the Father except the Son and those to whom the Son chooses to reveal him. (Matt 11:27)

The mind-boggling claim of the Church is that this is the one who became a man and moved among us in quiet and loving humility. Single-handed he fashioned a way for us all to find the eternal God and receive eternal life. He is the one who honoured the whole human race by setting up a Church of weak and fallible human beings to be his chosen channel of grace for all who come. To believe in the Church is to believe in Christ, who alone makes it credible.

THE CLOUD OF WITNESSES

The challenge of the eternal

The Church of the first Christians in its glory awaits us, and we turn aside;
the saints lovingly call us and we make little of it; the host of the redeemed
look for us and we are not interested. Brothers, at long last let us shake off our
torpor and rise with Christ to seek the things that are above, to set our minds
on things above. Let us love those who love us, hasten to those who await us,
and with our prayers come into the presence of those who are looking for us.

St Bernard of Clairvaux, twelfth century, *Sermon 2*

11: THE MOTHER OF US ALL

In Mary, the Mother of our Lord Jesus Christ, the work of God in creation reached its climax and perfection. For millions of years God had been preparing the setting in which he could enter his creation and reveal himself within it. For countless generations he led evolution forward until he formed men and women able to look on things as God looked, able to reflect on life, to be aware of themselves, to love, to create, to find ways of expressing thoughts and feelings in language, art, music, and in life itself; creatures able to value and rejoice in things that were good – in short, creatures in the image and likeness of God himself. He formed them to live in natural and continuous fellowship with himself. And then he watched patiently as they explored their freedom – and used it, as we know so well, to step outside their fellowship with God, and bring in alien ways that would trouble the whole creation.

He had allowed men and women to import a darkness into their own nature that was no part of God's intention; nevertheless he continued to work towards that climactic moment when God would enter the world himself, and fulfil his mind-bending plan conceived before the dawn of time. Human beings, left to themselves, could only expect to disintegrate in their separateness from God. But in every generation God intervened to plant seeds of new life in the hearts of chosen men and women, and so gradually to form the culture and the setting in which he could be understood.

Patriarchs and prophets found themselves called to trust God and respond to his guiding hand in ways beyond their understanding. Abraham, for instance, set out for an unknown country because God said so; he believed God would give descendants to an elderly childless couple because he had promised it. So Abraham became the prototype man of faith. A faith expressed in obedience and love became the route into God's chosen future. This was to be the way out of the darkness and into the new life God was preparing for humanity. To those who responded he poured out the grace of forgiveness, and accounted to them a righteousness that was not their own, but would be formed in them by the ongoing fellowship of their God. 'Abraham believed the LORD, and he credited it to him as righteousness' (Gen 15:6). So we find St Paul claiming Abraham as the *father of us all*, not only of the Jews, but also of all who follow Abraham's path of faith:

> The promise comes by faith, so that it may be by grace and may be guaranteed to all Abraham's offspring – not only to those who are of the law but also to those who are of the faith of Abraham. He is the father of us all. (Rom 4:16)

Again and again God took the initiative, calling men and women to follow the example of Abraham. He sowed his word in their hearts and minds; then in obedience they discovered something more of the depth of his love. Such obedience was always costly; for the world dislikes being reminded of its rebellion against God, and resents those whose lives show it up. But through the obedience of the few and the discipline of God's guiding hand on the whole nation, he slowly formed a culture that understood the language of faith, and would be capable of receiving the Incarnation of his Son in human life.

None of those called by God ever deserved it. It was by grace alone that they received their opportunity to respond and believe. This is what grace means: it is God's loving power poured out on those who do not deserve it, a power to trust and respond in loving obedience to his word. It is the only principle on which God will deal with humanity. The natural bent of the human spirit is to try and earn his favour. But this we cannot do; and we have to learn, as many of the Jews slowly did, that his dealings with us are by grace alone. Even so it was only a favoured few who could at this stage be brought to see the wonder of the grace of God. The full revelation of his grace and truth had to wait for the coming among us of his Incarnate Son.

Mary, full of grace

Finally in the Virgin Mary God brought into being the one who could be trusted with the full outpouring of his grace, undeserved as always, but finding in her a full and willing obedience that was suitable for the channel of his coming among us in the person of his Son. In Mary we see the ultimate realization of God's creative purpose. The First Creation could develop no further than this; this was its finest moment. After this the New Creation, with its new sort of life, could be brought forth – through the death and resurrection of the Son of God. God in Christ had to reconcile the world to himself at the cross, so throwing open the door of grace and forgiveness to all who would receive it.

It is impossible to overstate the significance of Mary. She is a human being and no more than a human being. But she is the crowning achievement of our God in creation and in the preparatory grace for his coming among us. Through Mary the whole human race is exalted to an unequalled place of honour in the universe, and through Mary we all share in the grace that was poured out on her and was then made available for us through her Son.

Jewish culture developed under the hand of God a special place for the *mother* of the family. A Jewish person was proved to be a Jew by having a Jewish mother; the father did not affect this. If your mother was a Jew you were counted a member of God's chosen people. This element of the culture expressed a fundamental spiritual (and biological) truth. You, whoever you may be, are proved to be a member of the human race through your mother; and she likewise through her mother, and so on back to the beginning. Through your mother you share in the shame of the human race in its rebellion against God. But through her also, by the same reasoning, you share in the grace poured out on Mary, the Mother of Christ. Through her you are a brother or sister of our Lord Jesus Christ, and an heir, if you will have it, of all he has won for us. Mary is, in a very real sense, the Mother of us all.

Protestants have over-reacted against past aberrations in Church devotion to Mary, and have tried then to cut her down almost to nothing. In doing this they have devalued the whole human race, and distorted the truth about humanity which Mary enshrines. Protestants rightly underline the awfulness of human sin, about which we cannot be too emphatic; but they do tend to make too little of the glory to be revealed in the sons and daughters of Mary. We, together with Mary, are intended by God to reveal to angels and archangels and all the company of heaven how great is the grace of God. We will not do this by ignoring the truth about Mary.

Fit to be Mother of God

The redemption won for us by our Lord Jesus Christ covers the whole human race, from the beginning of history to the close of the age. The cross of Christ happened in space-time as we know it, but it was also a timeless event, present and available in all its saving power to every human being who ever lived. On the cross Christ bore the sins of the earliest human beings, as well as your sins and mine and the sins of people yet unborn. Abraham, Moses, Elijah, Ezekiel are there in heaven because Christ died for them. God used these and many others in carrying forward his purposes for the salvation of the world; but anything they achieved was through the grace of Christ, though he was for them no more than a dimly perceived figure of prophecy. Christ was their Saviour, though they knew him not; and it was from him that they received the grace to step outside the limits of fallen human nature and do things that would have been impossible otherwise. God required their willing co-operation and faithful obedience, but the power to do his will came from their Saviour, crucified for them on Calvary centuries later.

The people of God were already a living organism united with the Christ who was to come, and depending entirely on him for their life and vitality. As he himself was to say: 'I am the vine; you are the branches. If a man remains in me and I in him, he will bear much fruit; apart from me you can do nothing' (John 15:5). No one ever did a work for God separated from Christ. And that applies also to Mary. Whatever grace and inward strength she required in order to be the Mother of the Son of God came from her Son still to be born of her. What she contributed was her willing lifelong assent to her vocation. Yes, she agreed to be the Mother of the Son of God. Yes, she would surround him with all the love and care that motherhood required of her. Yes, she would run her home under the guiding hand of her God, who alone could equip her with the wisdom to bring up the Saviour of the world. Yes, she would be totally committed to the unique role God called her to fill; and Mary knew she would receive from God the grace to do it. Mary's life was a perpetual 'Yes' to God beyond anything known before or since in the human race.

So we need to ask ourselves exactly what inward qualities were required for this impossible task (humanly speaking). The sinlessness of our Lord Jesus Christ did not depend on Mary. As Son of God, he could move in the darkest places in this world and remain untainted by them. He did not need a sinless Mother in order to be a sinless Saviour. But in order to be the Saviour of the *whole* human race he needed to take our humanity in *all* its fullness, complete and entire with no part of our human nature missing or damaged. This full humanity our Lord Jesus Christ gained from his Mother, and for this purpose *she* needed (by *his* grace) to be set free from the common heritage of original sin. She referred to her Son as 'God my Saviour' (Luke 2:47); she needed him as her Saviour in order to be free from original sin.

Inherited failure

Original sin is the burden of defective human nature that is transmitted to every one of us through our parents from our earliest ancestors. It is not in itself a guilty burden, because only *actual* sins that we have freely chosen to commit make us guilty before God. But neither is it any excuse for our wrongdoing. Insofar as wrongdoing is *unavoidable* we are not guilty; and God is well able to make allowance for this. When we confess our sins to God, we do not need to hunt around for excuses; if there are excuses there is no sin; and God knows this, and will not hold it against us. The things we have to confess are those for which there is no excuse; and we are not allowed to blame original sin for our failure.

Also original sin is not a genetic defect, though selection processes in a sinful world may perhaps lead to that – we simply do not know. Original sin is transmitted to us in many different ways very early in life, almost always from our parents. Childcare specialists tell us that there are many human functions and capacities that only come into being if triggered by the appropriate action of those who look after us; there are windows of opportunity during which we depend on right handling if we are to develop normally. For instance, a child deprived of smiles during a certain period in the first weeks of life never learns to smile, and so lacks a fundamental human capacity. Probably all our basic emotional reactions and drives are set up by mechanisms of this sort. They are programmed from within, but brought into play by interactions with others, chiefly our mothers. All the evidence now is that this process probably starts in the womb, perhaps very early in foetal life, as a mother's emotional state communicates itself to her child. The fact is that, because of defects in the intricate process of maternal care, none of us is quite 'all there'; and inevitably we pass these things on to our children. It is a mysterious facet of human development; and, precisely because of original sin, we shall probably never fully understand it. But we know it is there.

Likewise you and I will never know how far we have been saved from the worst effects of original sin by the providential interventions of our God. His love and care surrounded us from our earliest moments, and doubtless gave protection from many things – we shall never know. God *could* give total protection; but in his wisdom the whole human race is made to experience the bondage of original sin, except at the point of his personal intervention through his Son in the life of the world. Only through Christ is release given from the bondage of original sin.

To bring the Saviour into the world his Mother Mary, alone of all the human race, needed to have total protection from original sin. To be fully man our Lord had to grow and develop, both as a foetus and as a baby, just like any other human being. He had to see smiles at the right time, and receive the right pattern of emotional stimuli for normal development. If Mary's make-up had been defective or distorted, she would have transmitted it to Jesus. I think he would still have been *sinless*, but not *perfect* man; and so there would have been many human beings in the world outside the range of the salvation he won for us. Jesus must be the Saviour of the *whole* world; and so Mary had to be set free by the special grace and providence of God from the burden of original sin. Mary had to be all that a woman should be, for Jesus to be all that a man should be.

> To become the mother of the Saviour, Mary 'was enriched by God with gifts appropriate to such a role'. The angel Gabriel at the moment of the annunciation salutes her as 'full of grace'. In fact, in order for Mary to be able to give the free assent of her faith to the announcement of her vocation, it was necessary that she be wholly borne by God's grace. (CCC 490)

Since our human make-up is generated within us partly even in the foetal stage of development, this fullness of humanity had to be Mary's from the very earliest moments of her existence. This is what the Church calls the 'Immaculate Conception' of Mary. From her conception Mary was protected by special providences from acquiring the defects of original sin.

> Through the centuries the Church has become ever more aware that Mary, 'full of grace' through God, was redeemed from the moment of her conception. . . .
>   The 'splendour of an entirely unique holiness' by which Mary is 'enriched from the first instant of her conception' comes wholly from Christ: she is 'redeemed, in a more exalted fashion, by reason of the merits of her Son'. The Father blessed Mary more than any other created person 'in Christ with every spiritual blessing in the heavenly places' and chose her 'in Christ before the foundation of the world, to be holy and blameless before him in love'. (CCC 491–492)

This did not of itself make Mary sinless; but in order to sin Mary would have had to follow a path of deliberate disobedience, like Eve in the Garden of Eden. The rest of us, with our burden of original sin, drift *almost* inevitably into the paths of sin, choosing our own way instead of the way of God. (I say *almost*, because if it were *inevitable* then there would be no guilt for sin!)

A fundamental new start

The Church has always used statements about Mary as a way of presenting to the world the radical truths it has to share about Jesus Christ and the profound mystery of his being.

> What the Catholic faith believes about Mary is based on what it believes about Christ, and what it teaches about Mary illumines in turn its faith in Christ. (CCC 487)

At first Jesus was described as the long-awaited Messiah and the Son of God. But what did that mean? No! They did not mean that he was a god who walked this earth in disguise as a human being. And they pointed out that he had a particular human mother, just like the rest of us. So, was he just a rather special human being? No! For his birth was unique; he had no human father. So, was this a case of a god having intercourse with a human girl, as in the ancient Greek and Roman myths? No! The girl was a virgin who had no sexual contacts before his birth. So, was Jesus a semi-divine being created specially in the womb of the virgin Mary? No! He was the pre-existent Son of God who dwelt with the Father before the dawn of time, and it was by his grace that Mary received faith to conceive and to bring to pass God's eternal purpose of revealing himself within his own creation. Was he not then really a human being? Yes, indeed he was – more truly and fully human than anyone else, for he had a Mother fully equipped to pass on to him all that God ever intended a human being should be.

In this sort of way the early Church must have been driven to explain to the world the mystery of Christ. They started by pointing to recent happenings in human history. They ended by opening windows into eternity and into the heart of God, as well as into the heart of humanity. And the key to this developing theology was Mary. The Holy Spirit was promised as the one to lead the Church into all truth; and this was the route he chose to follow. The debate in the Church in those early centuries was wide ranging, but pondering the role of Mary was certainly one route by which the Church was led gradually to see the full wonder of the Incarnation. It was not until the great Councils of the fourth and fifth centuries that the Church reached a united common mind about the nature of Christ; and it was many centuries after that before it could see the real significance of Mary in the outworking of God's purposes.

We can trace the pattern of this development in the Gospels, and to some extent we can feel there the pull of the Holy Spirit that drew the Church on towards its mature understanding. In Mark (which probably emerged first) there are no birth stories, and we are reading just the story of Jesus, the Son of God; but in due course his mother is brought incidentally into it to remind us that Jesus was human. Then, in Matthew it is briefly explained that Mary was a virgin and Joseph was strictly a foster-father. Luke gives a full account of the events leading up to the birth of Jesus; it is in a very Jewish setting, and the angelic messengers make it clear to all concerned that here is Almighty God intervening in his world in a quite special way. Finally in John's Gospel we have the eternal Word of God made flesh and coming to his own people. This coming to his own is focused in a quite special way in his mother, with whom he has therefore a unique and unrepeatable relationship. John assumes we already know the birth stories, and when Mary first appears (in his second chapter) she already has a long-developed relationship with her Son; she is living at the interface between the divine and the human, and is pioneering for us all what this new kind of life means. She understands it no more than we do, but we see her quiet confidence in her Son. We see in her a simplicity of prayer that moves the hand of God. We see her example of unwavering obedience.

Later we see her at the cross, sharing without comprehension the sorrow engulfing her Son. Again she is at that interface between the divine and the human – where all Christians are called to be – on the one side the boundless love of God, and on the other the helpless misery of the human condition. Mary is there for us all, and we are called to join her. She receives there her commission – 'Here is your son' (John 19:26) – a commission to care as only a mother can for that poor disciple. And St John, obliquely but definitely, draws each of us to know with him that *our* commission as disciples of Christ is wrapped up with hers and his. In his Gospel he calls himself 'the disciple whom Jesus loved' (e.g. John 19:26); and so he invites us to identify with him as he retells the wonderful story. For if you are a Christian you too are *the disciple whom Jesus loved* – yes, *you*, loved uniquely and specially, with a love that Jesus reserves for *you* alone. So we too, all of us, are led to accept Mary as our caring Mother, and to join her in the task of loving all for whom Jesus died.

Our Lord, by his word from the cross, lays upon his mother the task of caring for ever for each child of God whom he loved. She was to become in a special way the Mother of the whole human race. Mary said nothing; but of course her answer was 'Yes'. Strangely, we find, as St John must have done in after years, that in her heart there dwelt above all else an overflowing joy – the joy of one whose life has been over-shadowed throughout by the power of the Most High. But the face she turns towards us is one of total compassion. She knows our need, and bears it constantly in her heart before the Lord. The task of Mary never ends; even in eternity she cares, lovingly and with joy, for all her children. One day the whole Church, living and departed, will be gathered to be with the Lord for ever. And Mary will be there to greet us.

12: THE HOPE OF GLORY

Human beings have great difficulty in talking about the life after death; and the Church shares that difficulty. The Bible assumes we survive death, but describes it only in symbolic terms (as in the Book of Revelation). Even the language of our Lord in this area is heavily symbolic. In the parable of the rich man and Lazarus we read that 'the beggar died and the angels carried him to Abraham's side', while the rich man calls out for help, 'because I am in agony in this fire' (Luke 16:22, 24) – powerful images, but obviously symbolic.

There is no way we can avoid the language of space and time in talking about eternity; and yet to do so is essentially meaningless. When we die we leave this universe of space-time; and to talk about the *after*-life and about *where*, *when* and *how long* it *will be* means nothing. For these are words that have to do with existence in space-time. John Henry Newman endeavoured in his great poem *The Dream of Gerontius* to show how eternity may have successions of events, but without the measurement of time. As the Angel says:

> For spirits and men by different standards mete
> The less and greater in the flow of time.
> By sun and moon, primeval ordinances –
> By stars which rise and set harmoniously –
> By the recurring seasons, and the swing,
> This way and that, of the suspended rod
> Precise and punctual, men divide the hours,
> Equal, continuous, for their common use.
> Not so with us in the immaterial world;
> But intervals in their succession

Are measured by the living thought alone,
And grow or wane with its intensity,
And time is not a common property;
But what is long is short, and swift is slow,
And near is distant, as received and grasped
By this mind and by that, and every one
Is standard of his own chronology.
And memory lacks its natural resting-points
Of years, and centuries, and periods.

We have an advantage in our generation over our predecessors, for modern science makes us face the problem of time even in this universe that we think we know so well. Distant stars and galaxies are not only far away; they are also long ago, for we see them as they were when the light that enters our telescopes first set out. Perhaps that star that shines so steadily in the sky has long since vanished in a supernova explosion, but we shall not know it for thousands of years.

The Theory of Relativity has shown that with two events widely separated in space-time we cannot even be definite about which came first; it all depends which observer is holding the stopwatch. Professor Stephen Hawking tells us that at the Big Bang, not only did *space* as we know it spring into existence, but *time* as well; and one day it will probably all end in a Big Crunch – *time* included. Even for modern science it is meaningless to talk about time outside the bounds of our universe – either before the Big Bang or after the Big Crunch. So our generation is used to facing the difficulties we have in talking about eternity using, as we must, the language of this universe.

God dwells in eternity; but he has also become incarnate in this world of space-time. The point where the infinite God became a finite human being, and the point where he returned again to be infinite God, are events that are always going to be beyond our comprehension. I do not understand how the infinite God could contract his being to that of a little baby – and before that to a foetus in his mother's womb – and before that to a single cell. But I do not expect to be able to understand it, for it is a place where the infinities turn up in the calculation. Mathematicians are quite used to infinity appearing in their equations; they know how to handle it, and they have a symbol for it. But nobody pretends he can *imagine* it! So I do not expect to understand the Incarnation of Christ: but we can talk about it, and see its enormous significance. Likewise with the resurrection: I do not understand how the finite human body of our Lord could be lifted from the tomb and so transformed as to be able to step into eternity at his Ascension. But we can say together in the Creed that it happened, and mean it.

The return of our Lord Jesus Christ at the Last Day to *judge the living and the dead* is another place where the infinities come up, and we can give no coherent description of that event. But we can believe in it, and believe also that he will raise us up with resurrection bodies like his, according to his promise:

> For my Father's will is that everyone who looks to the Son and believes in him shall have eternal life, and I will raise him up at the last day. (John 6:40)

> Our citizenship is in heaven. And we eagerly await a Saviour from there, the Lord Jesus Christ, who, by the power that enables him to bring everything under his control, will transform our lowly bodies so that they will be like his glorious body. (Phil 3:20–21)

We are citizens of a country we cannot even imagine. We really belong in heaven; and already our lives are being transformed in readiness.

Eternal relationships

Fortunately we are not obliged to use only the language of space-time in talking about eternity. We can also speak of relationships; and that takes us onto more familiar ground. It is one of the special insights of John's Gospel that *eternal life* is something that begins in a relationship with Jesus Christ, and (of course) endures into eternity. Eternal life is seen in John's Gospel as a *present* possession of the believer, not as something that awaits us at our death: 'Whoever believes in the Son *has* eternal life' (John 3:36). Note the present tense; and again: 'I tell you the truth, whoever hears my word and believes him who sent me *has* eternal life, and will not be condemned; he has crossed over from death to life' (John 5:24).

At the transition of death our relationship with Christ will be unchanged and will continue in his immediate presence from that point. We have eternal life *now* by hearing him and believing him, and this continues beyond death. Notice, for example, our Lord's words to the penitent thief hanging on the cross beside him: 'I tell you the truth, today you will be with me in paradise' (Luke 23:43). Clearly he expected to be in conscious fellowship with that man when they had both passed through the gate of death later on Good Friday. St Paul hoped to continue in fruitful labour for the Church *in the body*, but says: 'I desire to depart and be with Christ, which is better by far' (Phil 1:23).

The time factor in the transition of death we do not have to concern ourselves with. From the point of view of those left behind we 'fall asleep' until the resurrection at the Last Day. But we ourselves will have left *time* behind, with its weary ticking of hours and days and years, and will be immediately in the presence of the Lord. Perhaps we shall pass in one step straight to the Last Day and the resurrection. Who knows? More likely there are changes we must pass through first. But there will be no *waiting*, for waiting is something that belongs only in a world ruled by time. We shall pass by whatever route, long or short, to the point of resurrection, when we shall receive our resurrection bodies, which will resemble the risen body of Jesus – 'spiritual bodies', St Paul calls them (1 Cor 15:44) – and will reign with him for ever in the glorified kingdom of God.

For those who are living in a true fellowship with Christ the experience of death will be just a quiet moving into his conscious presence – certainly it will not feel like any sort of extinction: 'I tell you the truth, if a man keeps my word, he will never see death' (John 8:51). Indeed Jesus scorns the thought that anyone who belongs to God could ever die. When some of the Jews queried the resurrection of the dead, he said: 'Have you not read what God said to you, "I am the God of Abraham, the God of Isaac, and the God of Jacob"? He is not the God of the dead but of the living' (Matt 22:31–32). Abraham, Isaac and Jacob belong to God; so of course they are alive, because God is alive. The logic is irrefutable, and applies equally in our day to all who enjoy a true relationship with God through Christ.

The risen Mary

So God's purpose is that we should all eventually receive risen bodies – spiritual bodies, able perfectly to express and perform what our spirits intend. And what of Mary? In principle it was the same for her. At some point her earthly life came to an end, and she 'fell asleep', and passed most directly into the presence of her Son and Saviour in order to receive her resurrection body and reign with him for ever. The tradition of the Church is that Mary passed straight to her resurrection and ascension at the moment of her death; it is called her 'Assumption'. And why not? Protestants grumble that there is no scriptural or historical evidence for it – other than the absence of any tradition of a tomb for Mary at Ephesus (where she is supposed to have ended her days in the home of the Apostle John). But Scripture *does* have a tradition of a few special people being translated directly to heaven; Enoch and Elijah, for instance:

Enoch walked with God; then he was no more, because God took him away. (Gen 5:24)

By faith Enoch was taken from this life, so that he did not experience death; he could not be found, because God had taken him away. (Heb 11:5)

... and Elijah went up to heaven in a whirlwind. (2 Kings 2:11)

These are both enigmatic stories. But of course the fundamental evidence for a bodily translation into heaven is provided by our Lord Jesus Christ himself, whose body was raised from the tomb, transformed into the new sort of *spiritual body* he won for us all – and then ascended bodily into heaven. Is it inappropriate that this should have happened to Mary? For we are promised that eventually it is to be the pattern for us all:

Christ has indeed been raised from the dead, the first fruits of those who have fallen asleep. . . . But each in his own turn: Christ, the first fruits; then, when he comes, those who belong to him. (1 Cor 15:20, 23)

Why then do we have no reference whatever in Scripture to any such event? Surely the same reason applies as with many other stories mentioned only in one Gospel, namely that the people concerned were still around, and would have been greatly embarrassed. For instance, the raising of Lazarus, the greatest of our Lord's public miracles, is not mentioned at all in the first three Gospels; life would have been impossible for poor Lazarus if it had been; the story appears only in the fourth Gospel, written presumably when Lazarus had finally left this earth.

I think Mary did not like being mentioned at all; she must have realized all too clearly how easily she might come to be worshipped alongside her Son, and the thought would have horrified her. She preferred to remain entirely in the background, so that all the glory should be for her Son. Would that Christian artists of later centuries had been more sensitive to this point. Mary, the utterly humble but radiant figure in the background, must have been a wonderful strength to the early Church in Jerusalem, and later in Ephesus. What a pity the artists could not capture that thought! I reckon it was with great difficulty that St John got her permission to describe the wedding at Cana and the story of the two of them at the foot of the cross. And of course St John, like all the Apostles, was equally determined that all the glory should go to their Lord. I am sure loyalty to Mary would make him respect her wish and tell very little about her. We get the impression that statements about Mary were almost dragged out of the Apostles, and only when they were forced into it in order to protect the truth about Christ.

In this case the truth to be guarded was the resurrection of the body – of Christ and of every Christian. Mary received her resurrection-body visibly, the pledge and guarantee of what God will do for us all. Perhaps if protestants had allowed room for the Assumption of Mary in their thinking they would have given less space to liberal scholars who cast doubt on the very idea of resurrection, whether of Jesus or of anyone else. When the Church makes statements about Mary's passage into heaven it is stating what will happen to us all at the last day – what St Paul calls 'the redemption of our bodies' (Rom 8:23).

An intermediate state?

Christians have always wondered what happens when we die. If we belong to Christ – if, in the language of Revelation, we are among 'those whose names are written in the Lamb's book of life' (Rev 21:27) – we shall come into his immediate presence. That will undoubtedly be a transforming experience. All unholiness that remains in us will shrivel, as we come to see in the clear light of his gaze just what it amounts to; the encounter will be a radical re-creation, painful no doubt, but to be accepted joyfully. As the Angel says to Gerontius:

> One moment; but thou knowest not, my child,
> What thou dost ask: that sight of the Most Fair
> Will gladden thee, but it will pierce thee too. . . .

> Learn that the flame of the Everlasting Love
> Doth burn ere it transform . . .

> O happy, suffering soul! for it is safe,
> Consumed, yet quickened, by the glance of God.

But whether the process is instantaneous, or lengthy is a non-question; for we shall have left *time* behind. We cannot ask *how long* it takes; for there is no way of measuring it. In any case would we want to cut short a process that brings such blessedness? *Purgatory*, thought of as a place in which one spends a fixed length of time, like a sort of jail sentence, cannot be a helpful concept for our generation. *Purgation*, the purifying effect of entering the presence of our holy God, is something we must expect if we have realistic consciences.

Protestants resist the idea of Purgatory, since they distrust any suggestion of a second chance for repentance beyond the grave. The whole thrust of the Gospel is that *now* is the time for repentance and faith. To put it off is a dangerous thing, for there may not be another opportunity. To live as though we can sort it all out when we die is in fact to reject the Gospel. If we do not want Christ in our hearts now, we shall not want him in eternity. All this is true, and catholics do not scorn such wholesome Gospel teaching.

> We cannot be united with God unless we freely choose to love him. But we cannot love God if we sin gravely against him, against our neighbour or against ourselves. . . .
> The message of the Last Judgement calls men to conversion while God is still giving them 'the acceptable time, . . . the day of salvation'. It inspires a holy fear of God and commits them to the justice of the Kingdom of God. . . .
> In the presence of Christ, who is Truth itself, the truth of each man's relationship with God will be laid bare. (CCC 1033, 1041, 1039)

Catholics value the idea of Purgatory (even if the 'prison-sentence' concept is now out of favour); for they perceive the enormous gulf between the all-holy God and ourselves, and a process of purifying seems a logical necessity. Catholics are also fully aware that there can be no plan to retain a little bit of private sin; all must go, if we are to dwell with him in heaven, 'for our God is a consuming fire' (Heb 12:29). A confession of sin that deliberately avoids a full repentance is no confession at all. The Son of God has graciously crossed the gulf between us and a holy God, in order to bring us a holiness like his own; there are no other terms on offer. We must accept his plan now; it will be too late if we postpone it till we die.

But when our Saviour has done in our lives all he intends for this life, there will remain in most of us whole oceans of self-will, prejudice and spiritual blindness that will still need to be taken away. *Purgation* is a necessity, and protestants know this as well as anyone else.

13: DO THE SAINTS PRAY?

It is an enduring part of catholic piety to enlist the prayers of the Blessed Ones in heaven. It is assumed that those with a proven record of saintliness on earth must retain their love and concern for their fellow human beings left behind on earth, and will surely continue to pray for them. So catholics value tangible links with the saints, and celebrate their festivals, believing it to be part of God's purpose that we should see ourselves in a network of spiritual relationships that spreads across the boundary between this world and the next. This is a traditional Christian insight, described in the Apostles' Creed by the phrase 'the communion of saints'. We seek the prayer support of our fellow-Christians here on earth. How natural to extend this to include the support of the saints in heaven!

Some protestants are uneasy with the thought of invoking the prayers of the saints. They are by no means against telling the stories of the great heroes of the Faith, whether biblical or more recent, as a glance along the shelves of any protestant religious bookshop shows. They can join with catholics in seeking to profit from the example and witness of the saints, and in thanking God for them. But invoking their prayers is another matter. For this seems to play down our relationship with the Lord Jesus Christ, a relationship protestants rightly see as all-important. Outside that relationship there is no salvation; but within it we have everything we need in Christ. We may take all our concerns to Jesus in prayer; and prayers offered to God through Christ are all-prevailing. So what need have we of the prayers of the saints in glory?

Fear of idolatry

Many protestants are concerned with the danger of idolatry. Invoking the prayers of the saints can so easily slip into prayer *to* the saints that treats them like God – and that is idolatry. There is a sort of catholic jargon that is not helpful at this point. Catholics need to take care about this, not only because it antagonizes protestants, but also because it can mislead fellow-catholics. Protestants also distrust the painted images in churches and catholic shops, fearing idolatry; just occasionally that fear has been justified, when people are found attributing superstitious powers to an image. But in itself an image, like any art work, is just a means of communication – between the artist and those who see his or her work; if it is good art and fine craftsmanship it will say something to us. It is no different in principle from a written record or a piece of music. Even where it is not good art, the link with antiquity it provides may have its own special value for us, reminding us of the faith of our forebears. An old church building can serve this purpose in a community. Love of the building may be just an antiquarian impulse; but it can also be a route into faith and a way for some to find the love of Christ.

At the Reformation there was certainly some superstitious use of images that needed to be cleared up. But the wholesale destruction that occurred then was really just vandalism, a way for the violent to express their anger or the greedy their lust for rich pickings. The Reformers saw all this as an effective way of distancing the people from the old religion; so they encouraged it. This protestant over-reaction led the Reformed Churches to dismiss the communion of saints from their thinking altogether, which was a pity; for it is part of the reality God has created as the setting for our lives. He wants us to know ourselves while on this earth to be 'citizens of heaven' (Phil 3:20).

However, many faithful Christians still wonder what good reason there is for calling on the prayers of the saints. They claim to find all they need in Christ; why involve the saints? Catholics can respond: 'You may think you do not need the prayers of the saints, but you have got them anyway; for they are part of God's provision for us. Why doubt that the saints are still concerned for us? For God has made it that way. If you do not value the prayers of the saints, how can you place any value on the prayers of your friends still here on earth? At least the saints in heaven are able to pray with hearts unclouded by selfishness and sin, which is more than you can say about those who pray here on earth. By ignoring the prayers of the saints you cast doubt on all prayer.'

Actually popular piety among protestants finds plenty of room for the prayers of the saints – at least of our own loved ones, whether saintly or not, who have passed on. Well-instructed protestants are often deeply assured of the enduring concern of those who have gone ahead of them into heaven, and believe in their support at times of crisis; in my experience, it is the sturdiest protestants who are most sure about this. Perhaps it would be a good thing if protestants talked more openly about this aspect of their spiritual experience.

What is heaven like?
If heaven means anything at all, it must be no less than a direct and unclouded experience of God in all his glory. There will be no more need there for faith and hope, for these will be fulfilled in the beatific vision of God. But it will not mean an end to love – quite the reverse, for God *is* love. The direct knowledge of God will not exclude other loves; rather it must enhance them. In this life he teaches us to see and know Christ in each other, as well as by such direct experience of himself as he allows us. How much more will this be so in eternity. He has created human life to be a pattern of loving relationships, and he means this to endure into eternity. In heaven the scope for love will be greatly extended, not only because the circle of those we shall then learn to love will be much wider, but also because our direct experience of Christ will bring a new glory into all our relationships. Heaven will be a mutual

supporting of each other in love, which will make self-concern altogether unimportant; and this will be part of our immediate experience of the all-embracing love of God.

This love will also overflow in concern for those we leave behind. This love will be our prayer. Like all true prayer it will derive from the Father of us all, and be inspired and carried into effect by the Holy Spirit working through Christ. It will be caught up, like all true prayer (even on earth), into the eternal prayer that is the very life of the Blessed Trinity. This never-ending intercourse within the Godhead is the creative force behind all that exists – the word of God, spoken in the heart of God, bringing all things into being, and holding all things in being – and in heaven we shall be part of that. Even now on earth we are learning what this means. It is the *communion* (or fellowship) *of the saints*; and truly, as St John says, 'our fellowship is with the Father and with his Son, Jesus Christ' (1 John 1:3).

What do they know?

There remains the question: How much do the saints in heaven know about us and our affairs here on earth? How well informed are their prayers? We may well wonder whether they can know anything at all about us. For if they did, would it not spoil heaven, and disrupt their bliss?

First let us note that prayer even on earth is not always best served by detailed knowledge. When praying for a sick friend, it is probably best not to ask questions about the medical details and prognosis; such enquiries may be prompted by morbid curiosity rather than love. And where there is some moral failure we are certainly better not knowing the details. The saints in heaven would not want to know confidential details of our lives; and I think in fact they know only what the Lord chooses to reveal to them – and that will not be much. However, this lack of knowledge will strengthen rather than inhibit their prayers.

Here is an area where we must plead ignorance. We cannot tell how much they know about us in heaven, but we may be sure that God will not allow heaven to be spoilt by the intrusion of sin. It is my personal belief that the only bridge between earth and heaven is provided by the Lord Jesus Christ: he alone straddles time and eternity. When Lazarus lay dead in the tomb, he would not have heard his family or friends if they had tried to talk with him. But the voice of Jesus carried readily across the barrier that borders this present world, and called Lazarus back into space and time. In heaven they know what our Lord chooses to let them know, and that will be enough for their prayers to play their full part in God's eternal purposes.

The privacy of the soul

We live our lives in a network of personal relationships, in each of which we are able to share some limited part of ourselves. These relationships give us our identity, and reveal to others (and to ourselves) the kind of person we are. But in each of us there is an inner sanctuary of our being to which only God has access; no one else can know what it feels like to be me, except me and the God who made me. It is this relationship with my Creator that makes me an *individual*. Other relationships mark me out as a person of such-and-such a *type* – with this sort of temperament, that sort of background, and these sorts of abilities – and there may be many others in the world rather like me. But my relationship with God is unique and special to me, and it is this that makes me an individual.

If there is a sanctuary in my being for God alone, so there is a unique chamber in the heart of God for me alone; no one else knows God just as I do, and even I have scarcely begun to explore what he may mean to me. It is a creative relationship that constantly moulds my being and enlarges my capacity for loving, making all other relationships creative also. In this way each of us is able in some measure to reveal God to others. But our relationship with God himself remains always deeply private. The ultimate experience of God beyond this life will be eternally sustaining, for it will reveal to us who we really are, and the real meaning of our existence. But its essence is privacy. 'To him who overcomes, I will give some of the hidden manna. I will also give him a white stone with a new name written on it, known only to him who receives it' (Rev 2:17). The relationship of each human being with God is essentially private and incommunicable. This same quality is therefore imported in varying degrees into every relationship. We know each other, sometimes in groups together, but mostly one-to-one; and each sort of relationship is private in some measure to those involved. Some relationships are obviously so: husband and wife, patient and doctor; some allow room for others to join in. But in every relationship, if there is to be trust and understanding, loyalty and true love demand some measure of confidentiality.

All this is fairly obvious, when you stop to think about it. But I put it in this rather mystical way so that we may see that the privacy we naturally seek for our souls on earth is not just a result of being sociable creatures in a world like this. Rather it is fundamental to the way God has created us as individuals; and so we can expect it to last like this in eternity. Whatever else the judgement of God may amount to, it is not going to be a public shredding of our souls, revealing to everyone the unsavoury things that went wrong in our lives. God's forgiveness is more radical than that: 'You will tread our sins under-foot and hurl all our iniquities into the depths of the sea' (Micah 7:19). In other words he puts our sins beyond the possibility of retrieval, by ourselves or by anyone else. The only people in trouble at the judge-ment are those who refuse to accept such forgiveness; for then they are in the business of trying to justify themselves – and that way *every* detail will come out! And they will not succeed anyway; for there is no justification for sin.

His dealing with our sin is within the confines of our personal rela-tionship with him; there he will not allow any darkness to persist. There is a wonderful and loving confidentiality about the ways of our God with us, not only about sin, but about much else in our lives that we have no wish or need to share with anyone else; and the saints in heaven are too wise to want to break this loving barrier that the Lord erects around the inner sanctuary of our souls.

All through Jesus

A prayer for the support of Mary or the saints is a prayer offered through Jesus; it is for him in his wisdom to pass it on or not. It is the most nat-ural and wholesome of human responses to life. There cannot be any-thing wrong with the prayer of a child for a favourite aunt who has died: 'Give my love to Aunty Flossie' – and then off to sleep, leaving it happi-ly in the hands of the Lord Jesus. Those of us who are still pilgrims here on earth should live in the happy consciousness of belonging in the one Church with those we loved who are now with Christ.

> 'So it is that the union of the wayfarers with the brethren who sleep in the peace of Christ is in no way interrupted, but on the contrary, according to the constant faith of the Church, this union is reinforced by an exchange of spiritual goods.'. . .
>
> *The intercession of the saints.* 'Being more closely united to Christ, those who dwell in heaven fix the whole Church more firmly in holi-ness . . . they do not cease to intercede with the Father for us, as they proffer the merits which they acquired on earth through the one mediator between God and men, Christ Jesus . . . So by their frater-nal concern is our weakness greatly helped.'
>
> 'Do not weep, for I shall be more useful to you after my death and I shall help you then more effectively than during my life.' (St Dominic, dying, to his brothers)
>
> 'I want to spend my heaven in doing good on earth.' (St Thérèse of Lisieux)

Communion with the saints. 'It is not merely by the title of example that we cherish the memory of those in heaven; we seek, rather, that by this devotion to the exercise of fraternal charity the union of the whole Church in the Spirit may be strengthened. Exactly as the Christian communion among our fellow pilgrims brings us closer to Christ, so our communion with the saints joins us to Christ, from whom as from its fountain and head issues all grace, and the life of the People of God itself.'. . .

In the one family of God. 'For if we continue to love one another and to join in praising the Most Holy Trinity – all of us who are sons of God and form one family in Christ – we will be faithful to the deepest vocation of the Church.' (CCC 955–959)

It is right to express through Jesus our enduring love for those who have died; and we should not doubt their continued support for us. At the Eucharist we join in the same feast as they do – 'with angels and archangels and with all the company of heaven'. They are at the far end of the table where the light is too bright for us to make things out. But the same Lord presides at the feast for ever, and unites us with them in the bonds of his love.

Protestants may say: 'Those who are with the Lord in heaven no longer need our prayers; they have all they need. And for those who are *not* in heaven it is too late.' For ourselves, the language of finality is wholesome medicine; we should indeed be fearful of leaving this life outside the grace of Christ, for we cannot presume on having another chance. But for *others* we just *do not know.* What we do know is the obligation of love the Lord has laid upon us – and this will never cease. To the end of eternity we shall all need love; so how can we deny its expression through Jesus to our loved ones beyond, or they to us?

Many Christians feel deeply sustained by the love of the saints, not only of loved ones who have died, but also of those heroes of the Faith they never met, who lived perhaps long ago. It is easy to misinterpret such impressions, and of course we must never boast about them. But it can be a foretaste of heaven, where the love of God shared among all his creatures will be known in its fullness. To be sure, popular piety sometimes gets it all terribly out of proportion. We do so love to be sentimental; and it is a sheer indulgence of the flesh. But to deny or ignore the 'communion of saints' is to rob our secular culture of a witness it greatly needs – the witness of the Church to the ultimate spiritual reality that surrounds us all and gives meaning and purpose to our lives on earth.

THE SWORD OF
THE SPIRIT

The protestant challenge to catholics

The faith which the Church hands down to you has all the authority of the scriptures behind it. This is the faith, and none other, which you must learn to proclaim and in which you must persevere. . . . And as a small mustard seed carries within itself the potential of large branches, so the words of our creed are pregnant with the whole content of our religion as it is expressed both in the Old and the New Testament. Pay attention then, brethren, to the truths of faith now being handed down to you and write them deep in your hearts.

St Cyril of Jerusalem, fourth century,
Instructions to Catechumens, Cat 5, 12–13

14: HANDLING OUR MINORITIES

Rabbi Gamaliel was a wise old man, and experienced in education; Saul of Tarsus was one of his pupils (Acts 22:3). No doubt the teaching of St Paul, as he later became, owed much to this early grounding. Gamaliel was not one to suppress the original thinking of his pupils, or to want to destroy those with whom he disagreed. He was, I think, a better teacher than that; for he knew that, properly handled, young dissidents can become great leaders.

At this time the followers of Jesus of Nazareth were beginning to grow in numbers, and the Apostles were filling Jerusalem with their new teaching of Jesus as the promised Messiah. This greatly annoyed the Temple authorities, who saw it as a grave error to be resisted, as well as a blatant attempt to pin the blame for the death of Jesus on them. So they arrested the Apostles and brought them before the court, and were seriously thinking of putting them to death. But Gamaliel was able to intervene, reminding the court of several examples of recent religious movements that had come to nothing without any action by the authorities; and he went on:

Therefore, in the present case I advise you: Leave these men alone! Let them go! For if their purpose or activity is of human origin, it will fail. But if it is from God, you will not be able to stop these men; you will only find yourselves fighting against God! (Acts 5:38–39)

He saw that God often works through minority groups, who may for a time incur official disapproval. If a movement is of God, he will protect it and see that its message prevails. If it is not, then it will eventually come to nothing. Those in leadership have a duty to refute error; but to persecute those involved is both unnecessary and wrong. The whole history of the Jews illustrated the point; almost every significant forward movement had been initiated by one person – who was not usually popular. Moses, for instance, completely failed at first to win the approval of the leaders of Israel. The prophet Elijah was never popular, and the same went for most of the prophets after him; but God protected them and proved they were his.

So, said Gamaliel, if the Jesus movement was of God, he would protect it and it would thrive, and they could not prevent it; if not, it would soon come to an end. Either way it was pointless for the leaders to intervene. Let them get on with their own teaching, and leave the rest to God. Wise advice, Gamaliel!

Jesus and the fringe groups

Our Lord showed the same tolerant attitude. Reading between the lines of the Gospels, and from other evidence, we get the impression of a country in religious ferment at that time, with many small cliques competing for attention. The disciples reacted negatively to other groups; but Jesus would not allow it.

'Master,' said John, 'we saw a man driving out demons in your name and we tried to stop him, because he is not one of us.' 'Do not stop him,' Jesus said, 'for whoever is not against you is for you.' (Luke 9:49–50)

The unconverted Saul of Tarsus ignored at first the wisdom of his master Gamaliel, and tried to persecute the followers of Jesus – until that encounter on the Damascus road. Later he saw things through the eyes of Jesus, and was very relaxed about the work of other Christians with impure motives:

It is true that some preach Christ out of envy and rivalry . . . out of selfish ambition, not sincerely, supposing that they can stir up trouble for me while I am in chains. But what does it matter? The important thing is that in every way, whether from false motives or true, Christ is preached. And because of this I rejoice. (Phil 1:15–18)

False doctrine or practice in the Church would produce an instant reaction – as the Apostle's letters show. His method was to state the truth so plainly that it left no room for error. But this was the only way he ever tried to stop the mouths of those who opposed him.

We have renounced secret and shameful ways; we do not use deception, nor do we distort the word of God. On the contrary, by setting forth the truth plainly we commend ourselves to every man's conscience in the sight of God. (2 Cor 4:2)

Sadly, the Church has not always followed his advice, but has repeatedly used persecution as a means of enforcing its will; and this does not commend the Church to anyone's conscience. The Roman Empire persecuted the Christian Church when it seemed to threaten its institutions – no surprise in that. But then when Christianity was established under Constantine as the official religion Church leaders cheerfully made use of the secular power of the State to enforce their decrees. Whatever Church faction was effectively in control usually felt free to impose its will by force. During the Reformation in England both protestants and catholics were martyred for their faith; and so the pattern continued. In the next century puritans persecuted Anglicans, and then Anglicans tried to put down dissenters and catholics; and so it continued in one form or another, through the law courts if not at the stake, until about a hundred years ago.

Toleration in English religion is a very recently acquired virtue. We still find it hard to believe that our task is simply to commend ourselves to people's consciences *by the open statement of the truth*, and then leave it to God to protect his work in his own way. We feel we must *condemn* that other Christian group; and the effect is then merely to harden opposition. The open statement of the truth is a positive thing that invites agreement and affirms the alertness to truth we hope to find in that other person. The Apostle understood this, and it is surely the way of our Lord as we see it in the Gospels. There were rare moments when he used withering condemnation (for instance against the Scribes and Pharisees in Matthew 23); but then he was the Son of Man to whom

ultimate judgement was committed. He knew what he was doing; and I
have no doubt that at least a few of those Scribes and Pharisees were
shocked into repenting.

Children from stones

The ruling group, in any age and culture, always finds it hard to believe
it can be radically wrong. This applies in politics, at every level in human
society; and it certainly applies in religion. The establishment always
has difficulties with prophets – as the Scribes and Pharisees did with
Jesus. Earlier they had the same problem with John the Baptist. John's
task was to prepare the people of God for the greatest event in human
history, the coming among them of the promised Messiah. He called on
each person to engage in drastic self-examination and confession of sin,
and bid them all earnestly seek God's forgiveness. Many of the ordinary
people did just that under the impact of his preaching, and so made
themselves ready for the new commitment our Lord would require. But
the Scribes and Pharisees were not ready to admit that their response to
God was now inadequate; they were faithful members of God's chosen
people, the Jews, in covenant relationship with their God. What more
was required? They were confident of their status as sons of Abraham
and disciples of Moses. But John insisted that mere status counted for
nothing with God: 'Do not think you can say to yourselves, "We have
Abraham as our father." I tell you that out of these stones God can raise
up children for Abraham' (Matt 3:9).

In a sense this is precisely what God did when the ruling Jewish
authorities refused to accept Jesus. He raised up children from the
'stones'. He called forth a new people, some from among the Jews, but
many from the Gentiles, and set these up as his Church; these were to be
the new children of Abraham because they shared a faith like that of
Abraham (e.g. in Romans 4 and Galatians 3). When those in charge are
blind and resist his call, God is never defeated; he raises up children to
Abraham from whatever source he chooses. He is the sovereign God,
and is always able to protect the integrity of his Church, though its
rulers may in the process need to experience his severity.

All Churches have this problem when God challenges them. The
Catholic Church in particular finds it hard to accept God's lessons coming to it from other Christian groups. It is apt to stand on its dignity as
the Church on the Rock that cannot err; and it forgets that its inerrancy
is not a quality it possesses automatically, but depends on the continual
providential protection of God. Often the way God protects his Church
is to raise up an individual or group with a new way of looking at things.

It is the classic role of the prophet among the people of God. Prophets have uncomfortable things to say to the establishment, and tend not to use the right jargon. So they raise hackles.

Some catholic scholars do now talk of the trauma of the sixteenth-century Reformation as something God allowed in order to purify his Church. Certainly we can see the hand of God behind it. But let us be under no illusion that it was also a terrible disaster, which need never have happened if the Church had heeded what God was saying to it. In the previous century there were prophets a-plenty; but it has taken over 400 years for the Catholic Church to hear what God was saying through them. Eventually, however, God has his way, for he means to protect his Church from error.

A use for minorities

God uses minorities in the Church (or on the edge of it). Sometimes he may call out a small group to remind the Church of things it has forgotten. It is not easy for such a group, captivated by a lovely insight, to stay entirely balanced in doctrine; but some manage it. Their influence then spreads quietly through the Church, and brings new life and strength on all sides. In the end the movement fades because it has done its work. In our time much of the charismatic movement has been of this kind; and it has reawakened the Church generally to the role of 'the Holy Spirit, the Lord, the giver of life', and all he does among us.

Sometimes a minority group becomes unbalanced in its teaching, and drifts beyond acceptable bounds. What matters then is how the Church reacts; for it may be that, for all their mistaken ways, God is using them to prompt the Church about something. It is not our business to silence them; rather it is cause for the Church to examine and perhaps readjust its own ways. In recent years the healing ministry of the Church has been regained in this sort of way. Such a ministry first came to our notice among fringe groups, who seemed to talk of little else; this made the mainstream Church think again, and now the healing ministry is part of regular Church practice all over the country.

Gamaliel's insight, which the Apostles endorsed, was that a fringe group can be God's weapon to strengthen his Church, and we must not persecute it. We must keep it within the Church if we can, and then we may all benefit. This may not be possible; exclusion and separation may be the only realistic options. But even then what God intends is the renewal of the Church. And, if we follow the way of Jesus, the door will always be left ajar for the wanderers to return.

The planting of the Lord

Jesus and his followers were themselves a minority group, who often met with strong disapproval. Our Lord was always confident of the truth he represented and never allowed himself to be affected by a mere display of authority from the leaders of the Jews. He knew that his Father would vindicate him eventually – even if it meant crucifixion on the way there. If our consciences force us into a minority position, we must follow his example, leaving the final outcome trustingly in the hands of our God, and refusing to take up unfair weapons in our battle for the truth. Wheat and weeds must grow side by side for a time (Matt 13:24–30). God will root out the weeds in his own time – and we must leave that to him. 'Every plant that my heavenly Father has not planted will be pulled up by the roots. Leave them; they are blind guides' (Matt 15:13). This word of our Lord's affects the way Christians look at one another. We meet another group of Christians, who talk of God as Father, Son and Holy Spirit; they worship the Lord Jesus Christ as God's Son; they seek to approach him through Scripture and sacrament, and there is true fruit from their labours in his service. Above all *they are still there!* If they were a plant not planted by our heavenly Father, they would be uprooted. God works very slowly, and it might be centuries before we could be sure. But for the time being, they are *there*, and provisionally we must accept them as his. They may not be visibly part of the universal Church, and so we cannot join them. But we may not dismiss them as irrelevant.

Since the Second Vatican Council the Catholic Church has been firmly committed to regarding other Christian communities in this tolerant and accepting way.

> '... one cannot charge with the sin of the separation those who at present are born into these communities that resulted from such separation and in them are brought up in the faith of Christ, and the Catholic Church accepts them with respect and affection as brothers ... All who have been justified by faith in Baptism are incorporated into Christ; they therefore have a right to be called Christians, and with good reason are accepted as brothers in the Lord by the children of the Catholic Church.'

> 'Furthermore, many elements of sanctification and of truth' are found outside the visible confines of the Catholic Church: 'the written Word of God; the life of grace; faith, hope and charity, with the other interior gifts of the Holy Spirit, as well as visible elements.' Christ's Spirit uses these Churches and ecclesial communities as means of salvation, whose power derives from the fullness of grace

and truth that Christ has entrusted to the Catholic Church. All these blessings come from Christ and lead to him, and are in themselves calls to 'Catholic unity'. (CCC 818–819)

The Catholic Church accepts these other Christian communities as genuine disciples of Christ; but has it yet learnt to hear the voice of God through them? It accepts protestants as fellow-Christians, but does it yet hear what God is saying through protestantism? Any separated Christian group is a challenge from God – and not just to our love and tolerance. Their continued existence should make us stop and think. Do they reveal something the Church is in danger of forgetting? Or are they a nudge from the Lord to help us find new and fuller ways of expressing the truth? Or does their way of life show up weaknesses in our Church life? Or perhaps the Lord is calling us just to be more loving and build a bridge?

If we want to find the way forward in God's purposes, we have lessons to learn from old Gamaliel. It is a challenge to us all that we dare not ignore. What is God saying to us through the enduring presence of these other Christian groups – across the denominational boundaries and within each Church? We cannot just dismiss them as wrong. We have seen too much of protestants and catholics keeping aloof and ignoring one another, just as Anglicans and nonconformists have lived in separate worlds in each community, and just as anglo-catholics and evangelicals scarcely communicate within the Church of England. We have learnt to be polite, but are we yet listening for God's voice among the others? None of these Christian groups shows any signs of fading away. None has been uprooted by the Lord. The protestant Churches in particular are still there, and catholics need to hear what the Lord's message is through them.

15: THE BIBLE AS SACRAMENT

The main achievement of the Reformation was the rediscovery of the Bible as a channel through which every Christian soul may experience the touch of the living God. Of course this was nothing new in Christian experience. The records of the Church are full of stories of faith kindled and lives changed through the impact of some passage of Scripture. St Augustine is perhaps the most celebrated example, whose conversion was sealed through reading a sentence from the Letter to the Romans:

. . . not in orgies and drunkenness, not in sexual immorality and debauchery, not in dissension and jealousy. Rather, clothe yourselves with the Lord Jesus Christ, and do not think about how to gratify the desires of the sinful nature. (Rom 13:13–14)

And so he found grace to turn from his former dissolute way of life and embrace the forgiveness and discipline of Christ.

I wished to read no further; nor did I need; for instantly at the end of this sentence, by a light as it were of serenity infused into my heart, all the darkness of doubt vanished. (St Augustine, *Confessions* VIII, 12.29)

The writings of the early Church Fathers show that Scripture was the framework of all their thinking; and for theologians the Bible has always been the main source from which they have worked. The Church's worship and liturgy is almost entirely fashioned from the Scriptures, using psalms, extracts and allusions from both Old and New Testaments. The Bible has always formed the fabric of the Church's life.

However, in the centuries leading up to the Reformation, Latin had ceased to be the common language of Christendom, as it had once been. It was still a *living* language, but only for the learned; even the clergy were not generally familiar with it except in the liturgy. The stories and teachings of Scripture therefore came to the people second or third hand, through sermons, frescoes and stained glass; and that is not the same as hearing the *word* itself speaking directly to you in your mother tongue. To help the ordinary clergy in their job the teachings of the Church about human behaviour came to be codified in lists – of sins and virtues, works of mercy and fruits of the Spirit, and these in effect came to take the place of the Scripture in the minds of the people. In its structure this teaching was good, but it lacked the thrust and impact of the word of God speaking directly to the human soul; and it lacked almost completely the message of grace, which surely can only come through the direct touch upon us of the living God. In this work of the Holy Spirit the Bible has a pre-eminent place.

One of the earliest calls of the Reformers was for the Bible to be available in the language of the people. But this demand seemed seditious in the fourteenth and fifteenth centuries, threatening the stability of Church and State. So this opportunity to bring new life to the Church was lost. The general wisdom among the hierarchy of the day was that it was best to keep the Bible out of the hands of the laity for fear they would misuse it. This was a sad decision; and it still troubles the Church to this day. It was clean contrary to the true tradition of the Church, and it removed from the people one of the means of grace God has provided for us. We need *all* the means of grace; and Christian lives grow distorted when some are not available.

To be fair to the pre-Reformation Church there was some substance to their fear of the misuse of the Bible. Every deviant group in the Church always backed its particular viewpoint by quoting from the Bible. It is the same at the present day. Part of the general religious cynicism of our time is the feeling that you can prove anything from the Bible; so why bother with it at all? Christian orthodoxy includes a willingness to submit one's personal interpretation of the Bible to the collective wisdom of the Church. But the pre-Reformation hierarchy also had a less admirable reason for their distrust of the Reformers; they knew that the Bible would be used to challenge the errors and corruptions of the Church. Of course! And who can say the Reformers were wrong?

The role of Scripture
It is unfortunate that the Reformation led to a confrontation between the authority of the Bible and the authority of the Church. For in reality these are not distinct, because both derive from God. The Church has grown organically from its beginnings on the day of Pentecost. The Bible is a vital part of its early development, and a foundational element of its tradition, which it can never subsequently change or deny.

> 'Sacred Tradition and Sacred Scripture make up a single sacred deposit of the Word of God', in which, as in a mirror, the pilgrim Church contemplates God, the source of all her riches. (CCC 97)

The essence of catholicism is the continuity of tradition. Tradition can and must grow, as understanding grows and as the world changes. But additions that contradict what has been received can never be accepted. The true catholic tradition of the Church can never therefore negate the Scriptures; it can only hope to understand and explain them better as experience enlarges.

It ought not to be possible to use the Bible *against* the Church; but this is what happened at the Reformation. On the one side, there was a tradition that was trying to contradict itself, and needed to reform (which it eventually did); on the other side was a denial of all tradition subsequent to the New Testament, and an attempt to build a new tradition on the foundation of Scripture alone.

But undoubtedly the Lord was at work within all the turmoil of the

Reformation. The protestant tradition that formed then was bringing back to the Church a fresh realization of the Bible as one of the means of grace. For the Reformers the Bible became all-important; it was the foundation of their thinking and action. They worked on it and studied it. They looked to find in it the instructions of God himself; and when people approach the Bible in that way they find just how wonderful it can be under the hand of God. To those who are open to believe and obey, God delights to reveal himself through his word.

So the protestants were soon preaching not only the authority of the Bible but also its power and the need for a personal conversion based on it. They found the immense assurance that comes from a faith based, not on the word of Man, but on the word of God. This is the characteristic protestant perception of the Faith. It was nothing new in the Church, for the Bible was always intended by God to be one of the means of grace. But by the sixteenth century the Church had largely forgotten it, and needed to be reminded by the protestants.

Although the Catholic Church has now fully accepted these positive protestant perceptions, and recognized them as part of its genuine tradition, there are still many catholics who have never really discovered this part of Christian experience. They believe and trust in Christ, but on other grounds than his word in Scripture; and so they lack the assurance that should be theirs. As St John said: 'I write these things to you who believe in the name of the Son of God so that you may know that you have eternal life' (1 John 5:13).

We are meant to *know* we have eternal life. God would like us to be *sure* about it. Protestants can sometimes sound cocksure! We shall return to this in another chapter. But there is a quite proper God-given assurance that is part of the protestant witness in the Church. The protestant experience of the Bible is sacramental in character, and this is something catholics should have no difficulty in sharing. But to see this we need to think carefully what we mean by something being *sacramental*.

The sacramental universe

We have a God who likes to work through *things*. He can and does act through the direct touch of his Spirit on ours. But his preferred method – his regular way of working – is through things. He uses bread and wine at the Eucharist, for instance, and water at baptism. The sacraments are things God uses as channels of his life and pledges of his presence and love.

This method of working is all of a piece with God's revelation of himself through the incarnation of his Son. For our Lord was made flesh and used his human body to reveal fully and perfectly the nature of God, and to bring new life to the world. Thus our Lord's human body was itself the supreme sacrament – the *thing* which brought new life – and gives substance to all other sacraments. The sacraments of the Church are the main vehicles through which he continues his work among us.

The Church has traditionally listed seven sacraments, adding five other ministries to the two Gospel sacraments of baptism and Holy Communion, namely: confirmation, ordination, holy matrimony, penance and healing. This way of analysing the sacramental ministry of the Church was never meant to set limits on the Church's work, as though its actions outside the seven listed items were of lesser importance. Rather it shows that the active love of Christ expressed through us his Church embraces every area of life:

1. our calling in confirmation to serve him in the world;
2. our ministry, whether lay or ordained, for him in the Church;
3. our life for him in our families, or our calling to celibacy, perhaps in a community;
4. the way we confront evil for him, both in our own lives and in the world around us;
5. and our response to the suffering of the world he loves, and the obligation to bring his healing touch to all.

Baptism sets the seal on this mighty vocation, and Holy Communion equips us to fulfil it together. The list of sacraments was never meant to be exclusive; rather it includes the whole work of the Church through lay and ordained members acting together, by which the living Christ acts through his body the Church, to bring to completion his work of saving the world.

We live in a sacramental world, in which *everything* works together under the hand of our God to speak of him, and in which *anything* may be used by him to communicate to us his life-giving power and love. You can find such things scattered throughout the Scriptures. Let us pick out a few at random: the rainbows that God used to protect Noah and his descendants from the fear of natural disaster (Gen 9:12–16); Elijah's cloak that God used to bequeath new power and faith to Elisha (2 Kings 2:13–14); the mud Jesus used to bring healing to a blind man (John 9:6–7); St Paul's handkerchiefs God used to heal many in Ephesus (Acts 19:11–12). The list is endless of *things* that have been used by God to convey his power and love.

Almost anything can become under the hand of God a temporary sacrament – a *thing* used by him, perhaps just on one occasion, or for a limited time, or as a way of helping just one particular person. Most of us probably have precious *things* God has used in this way to show us his love or to stir our faith; they are important only for ourselves, and may mean nothing to others.

But there are some things God promises always to set apart as special in this way; among these are the sacraments of the Church. The Lord Jesus Christ is *the sacrament*, in whom God gives himself to us. The sacraments of the Church are the vehicles of his self-giving. His presence within them does not depend on us, but is guaranteed by his most solemn promise. We cannot see the Holy Spirit at work in baptism; but we can see the water. We cannot see Christ in the Eucharist; but we can consume the bread and wine, and know that we have experienced his vital sustaining presence. Sometimes it may be an experience we shall *feel*, more often not; but either way we *know* that we have met him, because he promised it; and we trust him to use the encounter to strengthen our lives. We do not have to understand it in order to benefit from it, any more than we need to understand the processes of digestion in order to benefit from wholesome food.

It is the same with the Bible. It contains information expressed in human words. But its purpose is to convey to us the touch of the living God in his Son Jesus Christ. It is sacramental in character, a *thing* God sets apart and uses to communicate himself to us – part of the utterance of God to his creatures here on earth. The Church has always placed the Bible alongside the sacraments in its ministry of salvation to the people of God – 'one table of God's Word and Christ's Body', as the Catechism calls it:

> Through all the words of Sacred Scripture, God speaks only one single Word, his one Utterance in whom he expresses himself completely . . .
>
> For this reason, the Church has always venerated the Scriptures as she venerates the Lord's Body. She never ceases to present to the faithful the bread of life, taken from the one table of God's Word and Christ's Body.
>
> In Sacred Scripture, the Church constantly finds her nourishment and her strength, for she welcomes it not as a human word, 'but as what it really is, the word of God'. 'In sacred books, the Father who is in heaven comes lovingly to meet his children, and talks with them.' (CCC 102–104)

The Church has always called the Bible *the word of God*. It is a name that makes the essential point – that here is the means God uses to communicate with us, and particularly to tell us about the Lord Jesus Christ, his eternal *Word*. But it is a name that claims very little else for it. Indeed you cannot claim very much for the Bible except that it is the word of God. It is not mostly great literature. Exclude Luke, Isaiah, Job and a few of the Psalms, and most of the rest is inferior writing – *as literature*. The majesty of some classic translations may make it seem great; but in the original it is not so. As an historical record the Bible is very patchy, and in matters of detail sometimes self-contradictory. It does not offer the scientific precision our generation values so much. It is a collection of ancient documents from a range of distant cultures, starting with ritual passages recorded first perhaps on clay tablets or sheets of papyrus, which have been edited, rearranged, lost, damaged, rediscovered, copied, reworked and tacked together with varying degrees of skill. But, having said all that, it is through *this* collection of documents that the sovereign God chooses to communicate with us.

At an obvious level the Bible is almost the only source of information we have of the life and teaching of Jesus Christ. Archaeological and historical research may amplify the information; but the Bible is the only significant source of it. The Old Testament provides the essential background for his coming, and was constantly quoted by him as authoritative. The New Testament alone tells us what the Apostles taught, to whom our Lord gave authority to pass on his teaching. But beyond this rather obvious function of the Bible in the Christian community, there is its role as God's chosen and regular means of communicating with the minds of his people. God can and does use any and every means of speaking to us – it may be something we read in a book or hear on the radio, a remark from a friend, a work of art or a snatch of music – all may be used as the sovereign God may choose. But the Bible he *always* uses; it is his chosen means of communicating with our minds. In this it has the character of a sacrament, and is to be used faithfully and regularly in the same sort of way. We may not treat it just as a source of ritual incantations for the worship of the Church.

Preaching the word of God

The Church has always used *the word of God* to describe also the preaching of the Gospel by its ministers. This usage goes back to the New Testament itself: 'And they were all filled with the Holy Spirit and spoke the word of God boldly' (Acts 4:31). There are similar references in Acts 8:25 and Acts 13:5. We also find St Paul thankful that the Thessalonians received his preaching as the word of God:

And we also thank God continually because, when you received the word of God, which you heard from us, you accepted it not as the word of men, but as it actually is, the word of God, which is at work in you who believe. (1 Thess 2:13)

To receive a preacher's sermon as the word of God is evidently to respond to the preaching as though to a word direct from God. This is how the early Church understood what had happened at the preaching of Philip in Samaria (Acts 8:14) and of Peter to the Gentiles in the house of Cornelius (Acts 11:1). We cannot claim that all our preaching bears a similar weight of authority – would that it did! – though it is not unknown, even in the contemporary Church, for preaching to be received as a direct word from God. But we are forcefully reminded of the fundamental importance of preaching in the life of the Church. By no means is it meant to be just a bland repetition of familiar thoughts. The aim of the Church in its preaching must be to open the truth revealed in Christ for the benefit of those who hear. It should come to them in the power of the Holy Spirit with all the force of the word of God. This understanding is an important part of the protestant tradition; and increasingly it is coming to occupy its right place in the catholic tradition too.

The whole counsel of God
We need to realize also in what ways the Bible *differs* from the sacraments. Sacraments bring us the life-giving touch of God apart from our understanding. It helps when we understand; but they do not depend on our understanding, which will only ever be partial. But the Bible works *through* our understanding. The words and their meanings are all-important; their communication to our ears and minds is essential. Those who translate the Scriptures know well how demanding a responsibility this lays upon them. It is the same for those who read the Bible in public: not only should it be read clearly and with meaning, and slowly enough to allow for a building with an echo, it also needs that indefinable quality that comes from believing that here is *the word of God*. Who knows whether the living God might not today use these very words to bring new light to the mind and heart of one of his children? When we read the Scriptures we are on holy ground; we are the mouthpiece of the eternal God. The Scriptures should be handled with the same reverence we accord to the Blessed Sacrament.

What God does with the meanings of Scripture when they have reached our minds is quite beyond our power to analyse. How he uses that simple thought from Scripture to generate new faith in a human heart is a mystery; and why the same word leaves another soul unmoved (who equally perceives its meaning) is even more mysterious. He stores up in our hearts snatches of Scripture with a wisdom and foresight for our future needs that leaves us wondering and worshipping. In due course the words and the images of Scripture come to be the stuff of our prayers and the means of knowing God's guiding hand upon us.

If you ask protestants to share the deeper things of their spiritual experience, they will tell you how God has used the Bible in their lives – how he has spoken to them through it and has guided their steps. Catholics may talk in the same way of the sacraments. But we need both Bible and sacraments, and we cannot replace either with the other. Protestants try and do this sometimes by treating the sacraments just as offshoots of the Bible – *acted promises*, they call them, to use a popular catchphrase. But if the sacraments could be explained in words, then they would be unnecessary. Likewise a catholic who ignores the Bible or treats it as subsidiary is also being false. Certainly there is a danger of misinterpreting it; and we need the authoritative Magisterium of the Church. But that does not make the Bible unnecessary for lay people in the Church. If God meant us to use only the sacraments and the teaching ministry of the Church then he would not have given us the Bible.

To ignore any part of God's provision for our lives is ungrateful and faithless. He has given us the Church and its ministry; he has given us the sacraments; he has given us the word of God; and he has given us the Holy Spirit to bring all these things to life in us. These are not dead formulae, but the means the living God uses to breathe new life into our souls.

> . . . the Christian faith is not a 'religion of the book'. Christianity is the religion of the 'Word' of God, 'not a written and mute word, but incarnate and living'. If the Scriptures are not to remain a dead letter, Christ, the eternal Word of the living God, must, through the Holy Spirit, 'open our minds to understand the Scriptures'. (CCC 108)

His programme for the human race and for each one of us in particular is essentially open ended. We would so like to limit his activity and confine it within a system we understand, but the infinite God will never allow that. There is something wonderfully creative about all his dealings with us in word or in sacrament, or in life itself; and we must never set limits on what he might do in our lives.

To neglect the Bible in preaching or teaching, or in personal devotion, is an act of disobedience, the same as neglecting the sacraments;

for we are disregarding God's basic provision for our spiritual needs. The Eucharist nourishes our lives, mostly at an unconscious level; and just sometimes we are gloriously aware of the Lord's loving presence with us. The Bible forms our minds and consciences, and equips us to handle life's decisions; it teaches us over the years to see things in God's way (which is the only proper basis for prayer), and builds in us a living faith. Then, just occasionally, God uses the Bible – or a sermon based on it – to speak personally to us, a word direct from his heart to ours, *the word of God*. It is an inspired name for the Bible, and for preaching as God means it to be.

16: A BIBLE CULTURE

Jesus was a *teacher*. His disciples often addressed him as that. Jesus also preached, but there are far more references in the Gospels to him teaching. Teaching has therefore always been the central role of the Church. The Church – Catholic and Protestant – still has much to say about education and how it should be done. But there is one matter in which we have all allowed ourselves to be diverted from truth and common sense by the spirit of the age – and that is in our perception of how a people preserves its cultural heritage.

Passing on a culture
It is done by telling stories. All over the world it is the same, and always has been. People tell stories – round the camp fire, in the market place, in the grass hut or igloo – stories about their past, and about their heroes; legends, with tenuous links to reality; fairy tales, with none at all; stories about the people in the next village; stories about gods and nymphs and spirits. It matters not whether the stories are true or false. This is how the culture is passed on. Stories live in our minds by mental pictures and images. Images simplify themselves to plain symbols, and these form the stuff of art and architecture, conveying far more to us than an outsider would ever understand. So our lives are surrounded by the sustaining web of our culture, and our identity is focused in the well-tried values of our ancestors.

Bad cultural patterns are transmitted in the same way. The hideous divisions of Northern Ireland or Bosnia are maintained like this – by always recounting and celebrating the atrocities of the past. Whether true or only partly true matters not; they serve very well for passing on the tribal identity from one generation to the next, and they provide the banners and symbols to march behind.

The Jews told stories, rather good ones, and so handed down their culture. Jesus passed through the universal human experience of picking up the culture of his people by hearing their stories. When he wished to set up a new culture, a Christian one, he went about it chiefly by telling stories – parables we call them. The Church has always taught the Christian faith by re-telling these and other stories – of the heroic work of the Apostles and of the early Church (as in Acts), and of the saints who have adorned the Christian life down the centuries. Above all we have passed on the faith by telling and re-telling year by year the marvellous story of Jesus himself. We have filled our minds and our churches with the images these stories generate, and marked our public buildings with their symbols. A single cross on the altar of a village church says it all, and has the power to awaken in our hearts the whole wonderful story of our redemption – of the love that brought the Lord even to this, of the weight of our sin that held him there, of the glory beyond and the grace ever-renewed at the heart of the community.

We worry greatly in our generation about our failure to pass on the Christian Faith. We deplore the loss of moral values and standards that goes on all around us, and we wonder what we, the Church, should be doing about it. The answer is quite simple: get back to telling the stories. It should start almost in the cradle. Before the age of two children can be told stories – not just Bible stories, but all those wholesome inherited tales that have formed our minds for centuries. We do not need to get snared on questions of whether the stories are *true*. Cinderella is quite frankly a fairy tale, but true in a beautiful way about all sorts of things in human life. The stories Jesus told are the same: there may never have been a real *prodigal son*, but the story is true about every one of us, and about the God who loves us. It is enough for children to be aware that some stories are in the Bible, and gradually to learn that the *truth* of these stories is a much deeper matter than they might at first have thought.

The Bible in the Church
Reading the Bible and expounding its teaching has always been at the centre of the Church's life, both in public worship and in catechetical work with the young and with adults. For many centuries this was done in Latin; for, in the wake of the Roman Empire, Latin was the one language universally understood in Christendom. By the Middle Ages, however, this was no longer the case; they had forgotten that the original intention of the Church was to conduct its worship and teaching in the language of the people, so as to be accessible to everyone.

John Wycliffe, one of the earliest of the Reformers, argued for the Bible to be available in the language of the people. In this he was undoubtedly right, and was correctly interpreting the real tradition of the Church. However, at the time it seemed a subversive suggestion, and an attempt to overturn an ancient tradition. Latin was the language of the Church, and people should be taught to use it so they could understand its ancient liturgy and Scriptures. It would never be the same in English!

In our day the work of modernizing the worship of the Church of England has met the same kind of opposition. Displacing the language of Cranmer and the King James Bible has seemed to many like a sort of vandalism. They realize that the language of Shakespeare is not really accessible to most people in England now; but for many who have worshipped that way for a lifetime the loss has been devastating. We are only 400 years from Shakespeare. In Wycliffe's day the Latin tradition in the Church was already at least 900 years old! It was unthinkable for the Catholic Church to change, and it would remain so for another 600 years. But the true tradition of the Church is, and always has been, to take the Gospel to the peoples of the world, each in their own mother-tongue.

In fact the Church never forgot its basic vocation to teach; and of course the personal teaching of the local parish priest was in the language of the people. But his source books were Latin, and he used them only with difficulty. And so the teaching became unbalanced. The story of the sufferings of Christ was always central, but only a few episodes of the story, instead of the full rounded account of the Passion. Before the advent of printing in the fourteenth century literacy was not an option for most people. Teaching was by word of mouth – aided by the pictures, frescoes and stained glass that adorned the churches. Like a children's story book, frescoes and stained glass could *remind* you of the story, but they did not *tell* it; for that you needed someone to read it to you in a language you understood. In the late Middle Ages there was a considerable growth in literacy at all levels of society. The printed primers produced for lay use show the extent of this. They provided a wide range of devotional material and prayers for lay use. It looked as though a typical English compromise might win the day; for often the primers had the English printed alongside the Latin. Most people still felt that *real* prayer ought to be in Latin; but all the same it was nice to know what it meant! It was a pity that the Bible in English did not quietly take its place in the same way alongside the primers and service books; it might easily have happened that way.

But the Reformers felt they were fighting a deeply entrenched sys-tem, and the only hope was to break loose altogether from the medieval pattern. So the opportunity for peaceful reform passed. Action and reaction produced the inevitable polarization of attitudes. Protestants severed all links with the Catholic Church and rooted out much time-honoured and wholesome practice. Catholics came to see the Bible as a dangerous document to be kept at all costs out of the hands of the laity.

Before long in protestant England the stories and images of the Bible were displacing the saints who previously had filled the imaginations of the people (as well as every corner of the parish church). This was a pity, for there was room for both. The saints had been an important part of community identity in fifteenth- and sixteenth-century England; they marked off the calendar and involved the whole community in the life of the Church. They gave a sense of the eternal at the heart of ordinary life. Our Lord and his Apostles, his mother and the saints, with our own departed loved ones, were all there, still with us through sacrament and annual ritual. We were one community, past and present, with a contin-uing life and culture to pass on.

However, all this the Reformers saw as part of the godless system that must be destroyed. Out went the saints, into oblivion went our ances-tors, out of reach went our loved ones who had died, and a thousand years of English community development under the hand of God went into the dustbin. It is doubtful whether English culture has ever quite recovered from that protestant devastation.

But again we can see how the Lord over-ruled to bring good out of the destruction. Before long the minds of English people, young and old alike, were being filled with the stories and images of Scripture; once more we would all be able to see what it meant to have a culture formed by the Bible in the way God intended. It is fashionable to decry the achievements of English colonialism; but probably the best thing we ever gave the world was the concept of a Bible-based culture. For near-ly 400 years English children had their minds formed by the Bible; and this cultural formula we spread all around the world.

Universal schooling was introduced only in 1870. Before that almost the only teaching in this country was by the Church; and that applied to what we now call secular subjects as well. The protestant Sunday Schools set up by Robert Raikes in the eighteenth century were primar-ily to teach children to read and write and handle basic arithmetic – to equip them as citizens in the modern world. They also gave basic Chris-tian teaching, and helped children use their Bibles, Prayer Books and Hymn Books. The aim was to produce not only literate citizens, but literate Church congregations, who could use the Church's printed material, and so be much more than mere spectators at its worship. The most lasting effect of the Reformation in England was to make the Scriptures, with the Prayer Books and Hymn Books based on them, the foundation documents of English culture. These things were built into the structure of our language and thinking from then on.

We need to rediscover our confidence in the Bible as the word of God. Our people are deprived, for in this generation we have robbed them of their cultural heritage. We have not passed on the stories of Jesus. We have thought that English culture was a matter of sharing political and economic institutions and the endless airing of views in the democratic process. We have allowed secular educationalists to declare the stories of the Bible to be boring – how did we ever come to let them get away with that?

I think the Catholic Church may be poised to pick up the protestant mantle at this point. For the Bible has an enduring place in catholic tradition.

'. . . such is the force and power of the Word of God that it can serve the Church as her support and vigour, and the children of the Church as strength for their faith, food for the soul, and a pure and lasting fount of spiritual life.' Hence 'access to Sacred Scripture ought to be open wide to the Christian faithful.' (CCC 131)

But the protestant Churches too have a long tradition of Bible teaching; I hope they still remember how to do it. We need to get back to telling the stories. They do not pressurize anyone. They do not have to be explained; Jesus very rarely did – probably never for the ordinary listener. Here is a task for all of us: to rebuild a generation that knows where it has come from, with a strong identity and sense of purpose, based on a Christian culture formed in the way God has given us – through the word of God. The most popular translation of the Bible ever made was undoubtedly the Latin Vulgate. St Jerome, its translator, had a forceful way of putting it. 'Ignorance of the Scriptures is ignorance of Christ', he wrote. The Reformation rediscovered this truth for the Church.

The Reformers were right. A Christian culture is a Bible culture. It is also a heavenly culture, and the saints and those who have gone ahead of us are still part of it with us. The Reformers foolishly banished the saints from their thinking. It is also a sacramental culture, through which the risen Christ is present powerfully among us; and the Reformers allowed too little room for this. There is a balance to be restored.

The creative word

One of the earliest and deepest insights of the Jewish people saw the word God spoke as itself a powerful and creative force that brought things to pass. 'And God said, "Let there be light," and there was light' (Gen 1:2). God created by just speaking his word. 'For the mouth of the Lord has spoken', the prophets could say (e.g. Isa 40:5); hundreds or thousands of years might elapse before the prophecy was fulfilled, but in the economy of God it was as good as done, for the Lord had spoken.

> As the rain and the snow come down from heaven, and do not return to it without watering the earth and making it bud and flourish, so that it yields seed for the sower and bread for the eater, so is my word that goes out from my mouth: It will not return to me empty, but will accomplish what I desire, and achieve the purpose for which I sent it. (Isa 55:10–11)

The New Testament shares this insight. It sees the word of God as having a life of its own in the community, and in the hearts of individuals: 'For you have been born again, not of perishable seed, but of imperishable, through the living and enduring word of God' (1 Peter 1:23). The word of God in the Bible is part of God's ultimate revelation of himself in Jesus Christ, *the Word*, as St John describes him. To respond to the word of God is to have dealings with God himself:

> The word of God is living and active. Sharper than any double-edged sword, it penetrates even to dividing soul and spirit, joints and marrow; it judges the thoughts and attitudes of the heart. Nothing in all creation is hidden from God's sight. Everything is uncovered and laid bare before the eyes of him to whom we must give account. (Heb 4:12)

Because it is the word of *God* it requires from us obedience: 'Do not merely listen to the word, and so deceive yourselves. Do what it says' (James 1:22).

God has always used sinful and fallible human beings as channels of his creative action in the world. The writers and editors of the Bible were people with the same severe limitations as ourselves – it shows through their writings constantly. Yet these documents have a quality about them that the New Testament describes as 'God-breathed' (2 Tim 3:16). You cannot say where the human part of the Bible ends and the God-given begins; the two are inextricably mingled together. It is all of a piece with the Incarnation of Christ. The human and the divine were always present together in his life; you could not in any way divide one from the other. The same principle extends to the whole ministry of the Church. A parish priest is even more limited than the Bible writers, and very far from perfect. But God uses priest and Bible to touch the lives of his people, and to bring to them the new life in Christ.

From the earliest times the celebration of the Eucharist has consisted of *word* and *sacrament* – both things coupled together – readings from the Bible with teaching based on them, followed by the Breaking of Bread in memory of the Lord, who is present and strong to save throughout. The Mass is the heartbeat of the Church, with its balanced ministry of word, teaching and sacrament. The priest's role in the community is to minister Christ to all who come, by faithful use of the sacraments, and by authoritative use of the word. The priest is the icon of Christ in the parish; by his life and ministry his task is to make Christ real to them, and to lead them into vital and life-transforming faith. By word and sacrament the priest's role is to help create a Christian culture, a fellowship in which God is real and faith is obvious.

17: BLESSED ASSURANCE

The protestant Faith that emerged at the time of the Reformation was a religion of experience. People had looked afresh at the Bible, and found there the voice of the living God, speaking personally to them of the saving work of Christ. Their faith blossomed, and they experienced for themselves his grace and forgiveness. In this way many protestants rediscovered the classic Christian experience of conversion. Their knowledge of Christ had come to them through the clear promises of God found in Scripture. Many of them therefore felt an unshakeable assurance of salvation; for God himself had promised it. They found a new joy based on the certainty of the ever-present companionship of their loving Lord, who, they knew, could not fail to lead them to heaven in his own good time. This has been a feature of the protestant witness ever since. A personal experience of God through Jesus Christ is held out by preachers as the objective of all sincere believers; it is a foretaste of eternal life, and carries the assurance of final salvation.

Here is another place where protestants have reminded the Church of something it was beginning to ignore – namely, the need for personal conversion. Catholics have sometimes suggested that this sort of personal religious experience is only for a few mystics and saints. But the real tradition looks for each human soul to discover for itself the love of God in Christ. In the Gospels it was the ordinary people who responded most readily to Jesus; and he did not mean them to be in the least uncertain of his power to save them. The *religious* people were the ones who found it hard to believe in him!

For some protestant groups having, or not having, the right kind of experience decides whether a person really belongs, or not. The statement: 'He's a real Christian' usually carries this sort of sense, meaning 'He has had the sort of experience that our group recognizes as a real conversion'. Nowadays, fortunately, protestants are usually more sensitive than this; they realize that God deals with us all differently, and that our assessments of each other are never wholly accurate. Our Lord's parable of the weeds among the wheat makes the point too tellingly to be ignored (Matt 13:24–30).

The brashness of protestant language may not be easy for catholics to swallow. But allowing for that, catholics should have no great problem with the protestant emphasis on a religion of experience. Catholic tradition is rightly cautious about people's accounts of their own spiritual experience, knowing how easily we can deceive ourselves. Visions and mystic experiences it assesses coolly, preferring to wait for the evidence of holy living and genuine spiritual fruit before accepting them at face value. But spiritual experience does not need to consist of visions and other unusual forms of consciousness; it is normally a matter of an inner awareness of divine reality that God may grant to any of us on occasions. And the ordinary *faith* of believers is itself a spiritual experience that the Church expects all of us to share at least some of the time.

Scripture has much to say about experiencing the new birth, and speaks in many places about the life-transforming effects of an encounter with the living Christ. The story of the Church includes many examples of people who have been suddenly converted. Pastoral experience in every parish turns up ordinary people who in various ways have found new life in Christ; for some it is as sudden and dramatic as for Saul of Tarsus on the Damascus road; others come to the same point of faith by slow degrees. Some fortunate ones seem to emerge from childhood never doubting the loving presence of the Lord Jesus in their lives. All these have entered into the new birth in Christ as promised in Scripture and as testified in Church tradition. We know very well that it should be like this for every child of God in the world. It is one thing to be baptized; it is another to enter into the experience which baptism is all about.

Revival movements
Christian history has witnessed a number of occasions when the Holy Spirit has seemed to move almost infectiously through a whole popula-

tion, passing like a fire from heart to heart. The preaching of personal conversion has always been a characteristic of the protestant Churches; and so revival movements have been a recurring feature of their story. Such events are not unknown in the catholic world also. These occasions are by their nature highly charged, and some such movements have gone madly off the rails. However, most revivals have been good in their effects, leaving a wholesome legacy of transformed lives and communities. Church authorities (catholic or protestant) usually find them hard to handle. Here is a work of God that is not explained by the human abilities involved; and yet because of the human factor there are things being said and done that are quite wrong. The wisest possible pastoring is needed if the fire of the Spirit is not to be quenched and the energies released are to be channelled for the good of the whole Church.

We have a God who intervenes in his world – most notably in the Incarnation of his Son. It is therefore no surprise to find him intervening in occasional events of spectacular revival. Pentecost was the first of these. At other times he expects his Church to continue the quiet work of teaching and pastoring and caring for the flock – and God is equally present in that. But occasionally he steps in to do something that none of us can explain or control; and so he reminds us that he is the sovereign God, and that we can do nothing without his help.

The best known of these revival movements in England was probably the Methodist revival of the eighteenth century. This started when two Church of England priests, the brothers John and Charles Wesley, received vivid conversion experiences. They were both learned men who knew their Bibles and their Church doctrine better than most; in their own lives they had embraced routines of rigorous self-discipline, and had endeavoured to live out to the full the obligations of being a Christian. Then, quite suddenly, the Holy Spirit opened their eyes to see that the truths they knew with their minds actually applied to *them*; and they knew in their hearts that Christ loved *them* and died for *them* to take away *their* sin. They knew they were forgiven, not because they deserved it, but solely for the merits of Christ. By faith in Christ alone they had received salvation; and even that faith was not their own achievement; it was a free gift of grace from the sovereign God.

They spent the rest of their lives in ceaseless preaching tours, and were able to lead countless thousands of others to share their newly discovered experience. They all found, sometimes suddenly, that God was real to them. His love became an ever-present joy in the fellowship of believers; the Bible spoke directly to them, and they discovered the power of Christ to transform their lives and to equip them for his ser-. vice. In short, they had been *born again*, and they knew it.

Where faith may rest
There was nothing new in the doctrine of the Wesleys. What was new was the way you were to enter the new birth in Christ. Traditional Church teaching said you were given the new birth in baptism. Wesley said you must repent and turn to Christ, and seek his Holy Spirit to enable you to place your faith in Christ and trust his promises found in Scripture. This also was traditional catholic teaching already expound-ed in the most authoritative way in the works of St Augustine and oth-ers. 'Repent and believe the Gospel.' It is the classic route into faith. But Wesley's teaching seemed at the time to conflict with traditional catholic doctrine on baptism. In reality there was no conflict. Of course the new birth is given in baptism; and of course it needs to be realized in practice in the life of each baptized person. The new birth is one of many gifts given to us in our baptism; and we spend the rest of our lives unwrapping these gifts and making them ours. Some people never unwrap them at all; their lives remain unchanged by the power of Christ and are still under the judgement of God, when they could be under his mercy and grace. But the gifts are given just the same, and will never be taken back, though they bring such people no benefit. Baptism is a sacrament; and sacraments demand a response of faith and obedience.

The faith of the Church rests on the absolute certainty of what God has done in Christ to save the world. This is a solid reality that does not depend on our understanding of it or our acceptance of it. It is a fact out-side us and not dependent on us or our culture. If the Church, the Bible and every human record were vaporized tomorrow in a hydrogen bomb, what God has done in Christ would still be a fact. Our faith may always be a wavering thing, and there are likely to be times when nothing seems clear to us; certainly our understanding of what God has done in Christ will always be incomplete. But that he has done it – done all that is necessary to save the world, and me in particular – should not be in doubt. Our God wants us to be quite clear about that. He wants us to be *sure*. 'These are written that you may believe that Jesus is the Christ, the Son of God, and that by believing you may have life in his name' (John 20:31). If we belong to the Lord Jesus Christ, if we are among 'his sheep', if we believe in him as the one who brings us salvation, then we can be confident that he knows very well how to save our souls and bring us to be with him in heaven for ever. He wants us to be *sure* about it.

My sheep listen to my voice; I know them, and they follow me. I give them eternal life, and they shall never perish; no-one can snatch them out of my hand. (John 10:27–28)

Foolish presumption

The only uncertain thing is whether I do in fact belong to him, whether I actually am one of his sheep. By baptism I undoubtedly have the right to call myself that; and no one may question it. And in baptism he has most certainly given me the power to turn to him and receive him as my Saviour; and no one may question that. But there is a question whether I have availed myself of that power, and have actually entered into that relationship with him which he undoubtedly offers me. Belonging to him, being one of his sheep, knowing him and he knowing me, is a matter of relationship. At that point the rest of the Church may fairly have its doubts; and there may unhappily be times when its doubts about me are very serious. At such times I may well be uncertain about it myself, for there may be little to prove, even to myself, that the decision I claim to have made for him is genuine.

Only the Lord Jesus is quite sure, one way or the other, whether I truly belong to him. If I am one of his sheep, he will have the means to draw me back in due course even from the jaws of hell, for he has planted a seed of new life in my heart that nothing can remove. But if I have never yielded my heart to him and am not truly one of his, then he will know, and will seek me sorrowing to the end – but he will never force himself upon me. The important thing is what *he* knows about our relationship; and, if I truly belong to him, I shall know it too, for his love planted in my heart will assure me of it. 'I am the good shepherd; I know my sheep and my sheep know me – just as the Father knows me and I know the Father' (John 10:14).

My relationship with him must be a real one. My perception of it may be unreliable, but his is not. I may lose my mind – perhaps end my days in senility, uncertain even of my own identity. But his knowledge is not uncertain, and our relationship depends at the last on that. For the Church at large, the only proof of my relationship with him is in the outcome, the *fruit* of the Spirit in my life. The mere appearance of being one of his sheep is never enough.

Watch out for false prophets. They come to you in sheep's clothing, but inwardly they are ferocious wolves. By their fruit you will recognize them. . . . Many will say to me on that day, 'Lord, Lord, did we not prophesy in your name, and in your name drive out demons and perform many miracles?' Then I will tell them plainly, 'I never knew you. Away from me, you evildoers!' (Matt 7:15–16, 22–23)

If he says 'I never knew you', no amount of posturing and quoting of Scriptures will mean anything; nor will a baptism certificate. To base our assurance on our own decisions is very foolish, for we do not understand our own minds well enough. We may think we mean it today, but next year's actions may show otherwise. The only proof is that we continue in the decision we have made: 'He who stands firm to the end will be saved' (Matt 24:13).

False assurance, based on our own estimate of our spiritual condition, is a most dangerous thing. True assurance rests on what Christ has done for us, and knows that by his grace we have received new life and a genuine relationship with him; this is much to be desired, and is most certainly what he wishes us to have. Protestants encourage assurance, seeing it as one of God's most precious gifts to us in Christ. Catholics talk too little about assurance, for they fear the false assurance that leads to complacency and closes the door on spiritual growth. But catholics then lose the deeper perception of our Lord's love that comes from being quite sure where we stand with him. There is a balance. There is an assured relationship, 'an anchor of the soul, firm and secure' (Heb 6:19), that makes us strong and effective in his service, and yet is sensitive and alert to the least thing that might damage that relationship.

There is no proper assurance of salvation for those who do not persevere in their Christian discipleship. But for those who do, and who seek to grow in grace and in the knowledge of Christ, our Lord provides all that is needed to guarantee them a rich entry to his eternal kingdom. If we use the resources he has provided for us in his Church, he does not want us to be in the least uncertain where we stand with him. He knows how to save us; and he knows how to complete the task.

Distortions of doctrine
The tension between protestants and catholics has led to polarization of attitudes in every area of Christian doctrine, nowhere more so than in the matter of the new birth. Such polarization always leads to distortion of doctrine, as each side tries to assert its position *against* the other; the truth requires both positions to be stated in balance side by side. Protestants shout that the new birth is received by repentance, by faith in Christ, and by trust in his promises; then, subtly, these things can come to look like achievements; and that denies the grace of God. 'Look how fully I have repented! I knelt down and asked Jesus to be my Saviour.

Now I trust his promises.' Oh, how proud it can all sound – my great achievement in repenting and turning to Christ!

But the sacrament shows the reality to be otherwise. 'I was given the new birth at my baptism, a fact I casually ignored for many years, though I was often reminded of it. I went my own sweet way, sinning with a high hand when I felt like it, though I knew perfectly well this was contrary to my Christian profession. I deserved rejection and outer darkness, but instead God in his mercy fashioned an opportunity for me to repent and believe, and helped me by his Spirit to accept it. He seemed to have always allowed for my rebellion, and now showed that his promises applied even to me.' There is nothing clever about trusting God's promises. Indeed, not to trust them is a sort of arrogance. Achievement, indeed! The only achievement in our salvation is Christ's. Well-instructed protestants know this perfectly well, but must not pretend to be saved *apart* from their baptism; for that is a distortion of doctrine.

Some protestants, knowing that the new birth is always linked to baptism, try and square the circle by saying that baptism should only be administered to those who believe, and so have already received the new birth. They avoid infant baptism, or else perform a repeat baptism for adults who have come to faith – usually by total immersion for good measure. But this makes baptism conditional on a profession of faith; the profession of faith is seen as the important thing, which apparently calls down the new birth upon us. So they deny the grace of God, and seem to make our salvation depend on our own act. Only the ancient Church practice of infant baptism makes the grace of God all important – a salvation offered freely by the sovereign God, with no conditions or strings attached. We have only to accept it. If infant baptism is the normal thing, the occasional unbaptized adult, converted and then baptized, makes the point all the more strongly. For such a one is accepted by God on the same basis as the infant, and must come as a little child or not at all.

Catholics are sometimes too concerned to protect the sacramental source of the new birth; and then they forget the pastoral need to lead baptized people into the experience that baptism is meant to convey. The Wesleys rightly put their fingers on this pastoral need, which was very great in eighteenth-century England, and is a matter the Church must attend to in every generation. It is not enough to tell people they are born again at their baptism. They still need to come to repentance and faith, and to discover in their hearts the wonder of what Christ has done for them; they need to be *converted* so that they begin to lay down their self-will and accept the lordship of Christ. Then, and only then, will they see what their baptism was all about. We are spiritually blind until we have repented and believed the Gospel; only when we enter a living relationship with the Lord Jesus Christ do we come to the place where the Holy Spirit can lead us into all truth.

There is a rich heritage of catholic practice that has evolved to help people make these vital steps of faith, and having made them to persevere in them. Confession of sin and spiritual direction to cure our blindness, seasons of the year and other occasions for self-examination, with devotional habits that call to mind what Christ has done for us and challenge us to respond – all of these are available to help bring us into the full blessing of our baptism. And fortunately in the Catholic Church there are many who take full advantage of these spiritual resources. But there are some who fail to use them, and so remain unconcerned and complacent on the sidelines. With lives scarcely transformed at all by the grace of Christ, their witness to him is only negative – they merely show how *little* he has done in their lives. Having no growing relationship with Christ, they lack the assurance of salvation that should be theirs; and the world around remains unimpressed and unmoved.

For a long time protestants and catholics have taught complementary truths about the new birth, and these seemed to conflict. But both are part of the true catholic heritage of the Church, and both are thoroughly scriptural, as long as they are held in balance. Both are needed if the Church is to step out with the Gospel in the confidence and assurance our Lord intended.

The role of the Church
Our salvation and eternal destiny depend entirely on our relationship with the Lord Jesus Christ. It is the glory of the Church to be able to proclaim this wonderful fact and make it accessible and available to all types of people.

> This is eternal life: that they may know you, the only true God, and Jesus Christ, whom you have sent. (John 17:3)

> And this is the testimony: God has given us eternal life, and this life is in his Son. He who has the Son has life; he who does not have the Son of God does not have life. (1 John 5:11–12)

The Church, by its fellowship, its ministry, and its sacraments, is meant to be the channel for the grace and love of Christ. God has left his Church here to be the vehicle of Christ's extended presence in the world; and the Church needs to be entirely self-confident in this God-given role. But it is *his* presence the world seeks among us; our worship and all we do is to be Christ-centred, if it is to fulfil his purpose. The Church has great authority, and has power to speak Christ's words of forgiveness and restoration – breaking the bondage of sin and restoring the sinner in the Church's fellowship. But it must never suggest that what matters is correct ecclesiastical procedure, when what is needed is a heart reaching out for the love of Christ, and assured of finding it through his obedient Church.

Our salvation depends on Christ alone. At the same time in practical terms it does very much depend on the support we receive from the whole Church around us. Faith is not meant to be lived in a vacuum; and our assurance of belonging to Christ is closely bound up with our experience of belonging in the community of the Church. If we cut ourselves off from that, our relationship with the Lord starts to wither. Even hermits need to carry with them the consciousness of the wider Church fellowship in which they have a place.

The good Lord wants to set our lives in a Christian community, the Church; and an important part of our salvation is learning to live lovingly and obediently in that setting. Love and obedience are opposite sides of the same coin; it is the coinage of faith, by which we express our confidence in the Lord and our trust in his provision for our needs in the Church. Love is expressed in obedience, and obedience is not difficult where love reigns. We are responsible for one another in this, and depend on one another. Together we create the environment for the growth in faith and love of the whole body. When that is right an assured faith develops readily, and doubt makes little headway.

Living this God-given pattern in the Church is a most healing thing. We know we belong to him and he to us. Through each other we experience his life-giving touch at every point in our lives; and such a lifestyle will always overflow richly into the community around us. The Christian life then seems effortless – and yet it demands everything from us. It is a joyful surrendering of our whole being to the service of Christ in each other. It is a foretaste of heaven. It is eternal life – knowing God through Jesus Christ in the fellowship of his Church. Even in the limited ways we experience this here on earth it brings a rich blessing of assurance to all who share it.

THE COSTLY TRANSFORMATION

The challenge for us all

When we call you tenderly to the unity of the true Church, we are not inviting you to a strange home, but to your very own, the common home of our Father. . . . We address all of you who are separated from us as brothers on the strength of these words of St Augustine: 'Whether they wish it or not, they are our brothers. They will only cease to be our brothers if they cease to say Our Father.'

Pope John XXIII, Encyclical *Ad Petri Cathedram*, 29 May 1959, on Peace, Truth, and Unity

---

18: THE LAST FRONTIER

Our generation is the first to be aware how small our world is. We know it to be only a minor planet orbiting a small star in an ordinary galaxy drifting in the boundless cosmos. Our earth is scarcely more than a speck of dust floating in space-time, and it is all we have. We have explored it all fairly thoroughly now; we have filled it as full as it will take with our species, and there is nowhere else to go. And this is the limited setting in which God intends to show us the wonder of his love.

At one time those who disliked the government or the social system or the religion of their country could emigrate and plan to be independent, setting up their own system, with its own economy and religion. There was always a way of escape for adventurous spirits; but no longer. All frontiers have been crossed and explored, and now the adventure is learning how to live our lives within the small framework allowed to us. The last frontier is the inward one where we must eventually meet each other. Across this frontier there is exploration to be done; and we need to discover afresh the astonishing creative resources of our God in such a venture.

The God of hope

This hemming in of the human spirit by the smallness of our earthly home shows up in the work of many original thinkers and creative artists in our day. Artists, musicians and poets always give expression to the inarticulate groundswell of thoughts and feelings in society. You may not like what they are saying; but it is our own aspirations and fears they are talking about. If you want to know what are the real undercurrents in the common subconscious listen to the artists and musicians; watch what they are up to. You may well find in their work at the present time a certain incomprehensibility! Unless your psychological make-up happens to dovetail with theirs you have no idea what they are saying. We always find it difficult relating to the avant-garde among us; but this is something more. For it seems they are making little attempt to communicate with us, the public, or with each other. They are engaged in an exercise of lonely introspection, from which colours and shapes and sounds emerge in a chaos that means little to anyone else. Do not blame the artists; for they are only expressing what is there deep in all of us. They know that the frontier we all face is an inner one; and they find there only a barren emptiness, full of despair. There is a deep depression at the heart of our society; life may be filled with ceaseless activity and effort, but this hardly conceals what is going on beneath the surface.

The Church all too easily joins in the mood of the world. A symptom of this is the small place given to the virtue of *hope* in the lives of Christians. It is one of the great trio of prime virtues, *faith, hope* and *love*, that Scripture and tradition set before us as the essential graces of the Christian life. Partly the fault is with the English language, which tends to use the word 'hope' in a rather negative sense. 'I *hope* it will be fine tomorrow', we say, when we half expect it to pour with rain. The New Testament use of the word 'hope' is quite different. It speaks of that which we confidently foresee and expect to happen. It is used of God's promises, of whose fulfilment there can be no possible doubt. *Faith* sees the hand of God in the *present*; hope looks to a *future* full of blessing. St Paul counts it the most positive of Christian virtues: 'May the God of hope fill you with all joy and peace as you trust in him, so that you may overflow with hope by the power of the Holy Spirit' (Rom 15:13). He wanted the Church in Rome to 'overflow with hope', as it placed its faith in the 'God of hope', the God who always has a wonderful future up his sleeve. Our God is never outwitted or at a loss what to do. The whole world may be in despair and feel at a dead end; indeed such a moment may be what he intends to bring upon us, so that the world may turn to him – if only in desperation. God has a glorious future in mind. Let the Church only trust the God of hope, and the kingdom of God will come.

For the Church, this last inner frontier is a goal to be sought; for this journey of coming back together is a long-awaited end. The Church is meant to be a sacrament of unity for all humanity – the sign of the new unity God always had in mind, and his instrument for bringing it about. The nations of the world may be forced reluctantly into co-operation and mutual acceptance, because they can do no other. But the vision of the Church is far more positive than that. The adventurous spirits, original thinkers and artists among us will not find this coming together a dead end; we must assure them of that.

For we worship the God of hope, who has a boundless future in store for us, not a dead end. We do not come together merely to find security and stability. We are engaged on the greatest adventure ever, and are set to witness the most original thing that ever happened – excepting only the resurrection of our Lord, with which it has much in common!

The example of Cuthbert

The Church at Whitby got it right and decided for unity, though it has taken thirteen centuries to get to grips with the rest of the agenda. For the Celtic Church it was a sort of dying; they had to give up their identity – all that made them different and rather special – all had to be laid down at the foot of the cross and given up. Christians think often enough of laying down their sins at that place of reconciliation. But more important is the casting down before the Saviour of crowns, trophies and achievements. Cuthbert and the Celtic Church found the grace to do this. And so they preserved for the English Church – for us in the twentieth century – the special things they valued: their reverence for the Holy Scriptures, their joy in a simple lifestyle, their burning ambition to spread the Gospel, their respect for nature in all its wonderful wildness, and above all the eagerness of their quest for holiness. These good things the protestant movement has indeed fought and died for. I think it would not have worked out so, had the Celtic Church clung to its identity and refused to come together with the rest of the Church; then we would have been the poorer, and they forgotten. As the Lord himself put it: 'Whoever wants to save his life will lose it, but whoever loses his life for me and for the Gospel will save it' (Mark 8:35).

Protestantism has fought the good fight – well, *some* of it has been good, anyway! – and what it stands for needs passing on to be woven into the fabric of the kingdom of God. But to do this protestantism must follow Cuthbert and the Celtic Church, and *give up its independence*. This is the way to preserve its life and all it stands for. To cling to a separate identity when God calls us to come home would be to lose all. The desire to be independent and not submit is strong in all of us; this innate tendency is the root of all sin. From this Christ came to save us; and part of the treatment he prescribes is submitting to the Church in his name.

The path of obedience is, and always has been, the only way to follow Christ; and always it is a sort of dying.

The way of Christ

Christians are rightly amazed at the Incarnation of our Lord Jesus Christ. That the Son of God should empty himself and take the form of a man, confining himself within the limited compass of a single human life, is remarkable almost beyond belief. It is even more amazing that he apparently felt *no restriction* in revealing himself like this. He did not feel hemmed in or hampered by the smallness of it. It lasted less than forty years, most of it in the obscurity of an unimportant town of Galilee. His public ministry took perhaps three years; and the record of it, counting the four Gospels together, with much of the story repeated more than once, occupies fewer than 150 pages in most Bibles. Yet this sufficed for Almighty God to reveal himself fully to the whole world. In one sense, the depths of eternity will not be enough to reveal God fully; but at the same time there is nothing more to be said than we may find in the Lord Jesus Christ. Here is the full revelation.

There is no evidence to suggest that Jesus found the limited social round of Nazareth irksome, or that he fretted to get on with his life's work as he quietly earned a living in the carpenter's shop. He knew that nothing better revealed the humility and gentleness of his Father than this obscure and self-effacing lifestyle, and he rejoiced that it was like this. He felt no frustration in the path his Father set before him; rather he found in it the same glorious freedom to love and serve his Father that he had known from all eternity.

Not the least of the revelations Jesus came to bring us is that God can be fully present and active in the small and insignificant. This is a feature of the sacramental ministry of the Church: he is present in a wafer of bread or a sip of wine, in a word of forgiveness or blessing, in a smear of oil on a fevered brow, in the union of man and woman joined in lifelong commitment, or in the passing on of an ancient calling through hands laid on a bowed head. To reveal God does not necessarily require packed cathedrals or stadium-filling crowds, or elaborate rituals and wordy prayers. He makes himself known in the small things: in the gentle service of love offered to a neighbour, in an insignificant life lived out in holiness, in the homely fellowship of a village congregation or a community committed to prayer. No child is so young and no person so unimportant but that the Lord Jesus Christ, the King of Glory, may dwell by his Spirit *with contentment* in their hearts, and reveal himself in their lives. We are none of us to suppose that our lives count for little in the world; the simple obedience of a childlike heart is always a potent weapon in the hands of our Lord. This is the way of Christ in the Church, and this is the witness the world needs above all else.

The Lord is not soiled by the closeness of his contact with us; nor is he restricted by the limited possibilities of our lives. All he asks is that we submit in obedience, as he did. He calls it *taking his yoke*: 'Take my yoke upon you and learn from me, for I am gentle and humble in heart, and you will find rest for your souls' (Matt 11:29). The picture is of two oxen yoked together, plodding their way in partnership through the day's work. So he links himself in a binding fellowship with us, in which he carries the major part of the burden. In this partnership we learn from him and come to see things his way; and the constraint of the yoke keeps us on the right path. The only requirement is that we give up our independence – which is what he came to save us from. The spirit of protestantism is a great handicap at this point, for it encourages us to attach too much importance to our own opinions and feelings. True Christian discipleship dwells uneasily alongside a spirit of independence; for always that spirit threatens to go its own way and disrupt the partnership of the yoke of Christ.

Belonging and obedience

Our Lord has bound himself in an indissoluble link with his Church, and with each member of it in particular. Protestantism has been right to emphasize the personal relationship of the individual believer with the Lord. His yoke is offered to each one of us, and must be accepted if our individual discipleship is to mean anything at all. But Christ also binds himself to the whole Church; and we cannot really take his yoke unless we accept also the discipline of belonging to his Church. Our claim to follow and obey Christ means little if we are not prepared to take a humble place in his Church.

The example of our Lord Jesus Christ should settle the matter for us. It is a familiar truth that he was continually obedient to his heavenly Father. But when it was appropriate he was also obedient to other human beings and human institutions for his Father's sake. At the age of twelve, when a Jewish boy took personal responsibility for his own actions, he stayed behind in the Temple, 'sitting among the teachers, listening to them and asking them questions' (Luke 2:46). He accepted the humble role of a student; and then at the end of that story we see him submit to his parents: 'he went down to Nazareth with them and was obedient to them' (Luke 2:51). We also see him throughout his life quietly accepting Jewish law and customs, and joining in the forms of worship of Temple and synagogue. When legalism obscured the spirit of the law he could brush aside a silly man-made rule. But in the normal way he knew that obedience to his Father required submission to human institutions and customs; and he accepted the 'Church' of the Jews as his Father's creation to which he was subject. If we mean to follow Christ we too must accept human rules within the framework of his Church. The occasions when it is right to resist will be very few.

Our Lord submitted to his Father's will, even when it led to the cross. He found nothing constricting or hampering in this; rather it was the opportunity to express his freedom to be truly the Son of God. In the same way we must submit to his will – which includes being subject to his Church – and, like him, be prepared for the best we have to be cru-cified in his service. He comes to share with us his own unfettered free-dom – the freedom to be all that God means us to be. And the way to step out into that freedom is to take his yoke and join ourselves to the Church for which he gave his life.

19: FREEING THE LOG-JAM

Without doubt the greatest obstacle to the coming together of Chris-tians in England is just habit and inertia. The logs are jammed in the river in a particular way; we understand the pattern, and are used to it. We know where we belong in it, and are happy for things to stay as they are. There is an uneasy stability about the English Church scene. But this consensus is more in being English, the product of a shared histor-ical process, than in being members of the Church. I do not believe the Lord will allow this pseudo-stability, this polite divergence, to continue. For it makes our witness to the English people a sham. Instead of a uni-versal Church proclaiming the Gospel of the Incarnate God to the whole world, we have substituted a collection of English social tradi-tions with an appeal that reaches little beyond their own cultural circles. For most Christians in England (in *all* the Churches), vision is limited to keeping their own show going, in place of the boundless panorama of growth and transformation left us by the Apostles.

Recent events in the Church of England have shifted the logs in a fundamental way, and the whole tangle is starting to move once more down the river towards the open water. The Lord is pushing us all into new relationships, and nothing will ever be the same again. The door to God's future is opening, and we should not even try to shut it. It is one of those times of change when the only safety for any Christian is in a close walk with Christ. We need to be alert to the moving of the Spirit and not allow ourselves to stagnate in a backwater.

Being universal Christians

The Catholic Church in England is part of the log-jam too, with its own neat and accepted place within it; and it too seems a little nervous of the present shifting pattern of Church life in England. But the Catholic Church has the special calling of holding before us all the majestic vision of a *universal* Church. Thank God it has shed its triumphalist image, which helped no one. But we do need it to be more than just parochial. For it is *foundational* and *basic*, the only possible meeting point for all true strands of the Faith. Christianity in England needs a new focus, in which our people will recognize once more the authentic apostolic voice. Where will they find it if not in the Catholic Church?

Sometimes the Catholic Church has given the impression of being monolithic, unchanging and unchangeable. This of course is an illusion. It has been constantly developing throughout its history in response to the pressures of the world around and its own internal debates; and its style has always adapted to different communities and cultures in all the diverse ways human life seems to require. Being founded on the rock does not mean never changing; quite the reverse, for it requires a constant sensitivity to the Holy Spirit, who is always at work, through human pressures, and through his own impact in our hearts, to produce new life and growth.

The basic foundation of the Church is Jesus Christ; there can be no other (1 Cor 3:11). Then, by his will, on that foundation we have the secondary foundation of Peter and the Apostles (Eph 2:20). That cannot change. But we have an ever-creative God, who will always be fashioning bright new designs for his Church, bringing new life in place of stagnation and death. Always the new patterns will agree with the old, but will never just repeat them. Being built on an apostolic foundation, commits us to a programme of continual growth and development. We need a sort of bubbling joy to match (if that were possible) the astonishing creativity of our God.

> Oh, the depth of the riches of the wisdom and knowledge of God! How unsearchable his judgments, and his paths beyond tracing out! 'Who has known the mind of the Lord? Or who has been his counsellor?' (Rom 11:33–36, quoting Isa 40:13)

St Paul looked deeper into the future than most of us; and it left him blinking with amazement as he peered toward the distant horizon of God's purposes.

There is a striking contrast between the forward-looking vision of the Apostle and the absence of any such thing in most Church circles. Christians seem to be busy in their various ways trying to mould the Church to the patterns of the world, trying to speak to our contemporaries in their own language, trying to adapt the Church to suit them, and to make them feel comfortable when they cross the threshold. But at the heart of the apostolic tradition there is a glorious hope, a hope that challenges the world and bids it learn how to follow Christ and shed its own futile programmes.

At the local level the Catholic Church may look and feel much the same as any other Church. It has its advertised services and events, its buildings and ministers, its fund-raising efforts, its committees and working parties – just like everyone else. But it has one quality that sets it apart from all the others, namely its *catholicity*. It is, by its very nature, universal and continuous, down the centuries and all over the world – continuous with the Church of the Apostles, as well as with the Church in glory. Other Churches value significant links with the Apostles, through the Scriptures and through their historical origins. But the Catholic Church is the only Church that has total continuity with the Apostolic Church, and so is universal; it is the only *catholic* Church.

Its inner life therefore carries within it the all-embracing vision of a world being transformed under the creative hand of God, with the Church as his instrument, as he makes the glory of Jesus blossom in communities of ordinary men and women, and makes the love of Jesus a reality sustaining the rich diversity of his world. We all need to discover how to be *universal* Christians; and there is only one way of doing this, namely by being *catholic* Christians – the words mean the same thing. You can belong to Christ in another Church, but you cannot be in the centre of his purposes unless you share the high vision he has set before us of all humanity united in his Church.

I believe the Lord has fashioned a moment when the barriers that separate catholic and protestant can be looked at with new eyes. It is all part of a much wider programme of uniting the whole human race.

Now in Christ Jesus you who once were far away have been brought near through the blood of Christ. For he himself is our peace, who has made the two one and has destroyed the barrier, the dividing wall of hostility. . . . His purpose was to create in himself one new man out of the two, thus making peace. (Eph 2:13–15)

St Paul wrote these words about a far greater barrier, namely that between Jew and Gentile. Compared with that the protestant–catholic divide is trivial. If Christ brought to an end that ancient division of Gentile and Jew, how much more readily can he bring together us Christians parted by a mere 400 years of history.

Ending the schism

I doubt whether we should look for any more progress from big corporate schemes of Church reunion. There have been a few of these; and some have helped bring Christians together. But the problem is that such schemes depend on negotiation; and truth is not arrived at by any sort of bargaining process. This only produces ambiguous statements that speak differently to different people. Besides, it never convinces those who were not party to the discussions. David Edwards in *What is Catholicism?* attempts, as it were, to reopen the negotiations (of ARCIC for instance). It is good when Christians who differ can talk together. But it does not let us off the obligation to come together. However much we talk there will always remain the problem of reconciling two different religions, the protestant and the catholic, when one of them wants to retain the freedom to be different. More is achieved when Christians share in each other's spirituality, and so experience true worship in new and unfamiliar ways. In the end the only way to decide whether to become a catholic is to join in and find what it is like from the inside.

It is time the protestant schism was brought to an end. It may once have served a purpose in helping the Church to reform; but it serves that purpose no longer. There is now no good reason to stay apart. The fact is that protestants have grown so accustomed to their independence that they can scarcely imagine being part of a wider unity.

For the Church of England this is particularly difficult. It is surrounded with a panoply of ancient forms and ceremonies and buildings, and has a long-established place in English society at every level from the palace to the village street. It is built into our constitutional monarchy and parliamentary democracy, and seems as permanent and solid as anything else in our national life. But this solidity is an illusion, for it depends simply on being English. I am proud of my country and its achievements, and the heritage of good sense it has bequeathed to the world, but mere Englishness is no foundation on which to build the Church of God. I believe the Church of England has been used by God in wonderful ways to preserve for the whole Church things it was in danger of forgetting. But by its nature it has always tended to respond too much to English social needs and too little to the eternal truths revealed in Christ. As a result its structure, which appears so stable and reliable, is really hollow, and always open to inroads from worldly pressures.

Its bishops are not catholic bishops, however lengthy their pedigrees. They unite the Church only as far as it wants to be united – which is not much! They are not guardians of its doctrine; for its members are free to pick and choose the teaching they like, and can probably find support somewhere among the clergy for almost any doctrine or practice you care to name. It is the same with its services and patterns of worship: shop around, and suit your fancy, is the general message to its members. It is a tolerant body that has learnt to fit in easily with the English social scene. It belongs in the world of Trollope and Parson Woodforde and all the other characters, real and fictional, ancient and modern, that engage the imaginations of the English. Some of its leaders have been fine and saintly people; but mostly they are just very English, and that is how English people like it.

The Church of England has long been an unquestioned part of our national identity. (But in a time of total upheaval such as we are now passing through, can it play that role any longer?) It often imparts a comfortable feeling of divine authority to essentially English decisions, both nationally and in the Church. And like all other English institutions we never let ourselves take it too seriously! The English have fashioned a Church in their own image, and so made sure that it poses no challenge to their way of life. I suppose every nation tries to do this in its own way, seeking to tame the Church to suit its national temperament. That is why we must have a *universal* Church that transcends national boundaries and limitations. We need a Church that speaks with authority from beyond our national consciousness. And this is exactly what the Lord has provided for us in the Catholic Church.

This is not to say that the Church of England and the other protestant Churches lack all spiritual authority. Far from it! When they teach from the Scriptures and when they employ ancient forms of worship and spirituality, there is a great weight of authority behind them, particularly when those who minister are faithful followers of Christ and are able to speak from the heart about him. However, the authority they wield is not inherently theirs, but derives rather from the Scriptures and from the ancient Church they have invoked. What people perceive in their ministry is really an authority reflected from the universal Church, as first set up by Christ. Protestant ministers are sprinkled, as it were, with light from the apostolic torch – even while they deny its real source in the universal Church. So there is inevitably an element of make-believe in the ministry of protestants; they are putting on a show of ministerial authority without its substance; the substance belongs elsewhere. None are better at doing this than ministers of the Church of England. But it is a sham; and many of the clergy simply cannot any longer really believe in their own authority.

True authority belongs with those who are acting in obedience within the Church that Christ set up to be his witness in the world. The centurion who sought our Lord's help in the Gospels understood this point perfectly:

> 'Lord, I do not deserve to have you come under my roof. But just say the word, and my servant will be healed. For I myself am a man under authority, with soldiers under me.' (Matt 8:8–9)

That Roman officer recognized in Jesus someone who, like himself, was *in* authority because he was *under* authority – in Jesus' case the authority of his Father. The authority of the universal Church rests with its obedient servants. The validity of their orders depends on their continuing relationship of love and obedience within the Church, a relationship stretching back to Christ and his Apostles.

The protestant Churches recognize the authority of the Scriptures, but lack the Magisterium for assessing the truth that belongs with it. In practice they must take their decisions and derive their working authority from the consent of their members, expressed through synods and committees. It is a democratic procedure that seems acceptable to our generation. But a democratic vote is no more than a way for a group of human beings to decide on a course of action. It can never settle issues of eternal truth. The protestant Churches, however, continue to insist on taking votes on such matters – for there is nothing else they can do. And so they encourage and perpetuate the modern notion that truth is a matter of opinion. We all know perfectly well that the votes they take settle nothing. The truth about the ultimate issues of life is to be found in God, and is revealed in Christ. It may be difficult to uncover; but it is not a matter of opinion at all.

Protestant synods may sincerely seek the guidance of the Holy Spirit in their decision-making, but their votes provide no guarantee that they have found it. Indeed if the pressure of the Holy Spirit in our time is all towards reuniting the disciples of Christ in the universal Church, then the prayers of protestants for guidance count for very little until they start to respond to that pressure.

I suppose it is just possible that some protestant Churches might take a democratic decision to rejoin the universal Church. But I do not think it very likely; and even if they did, it would not count for anything, for dissenting members would not accept the decision; and there is no reason why they should. The way forward must be for individual people to make their decisions – countless numbers of them – for love of the Lord and in obedience to his revealed will. We come into a true relationship with Christ's Church one-by-one, sheep-by-sheep, lamb-by-lamb. This is the path, taken by individuals and families and groups of Christian friends, that needs to be followed by all who have glimpsed the universal prospect God sets before us.

Protestants are inclined to reason that the way God has richly blessed their work and ministry proves that they are already basically on the right lines. But all it proves is the graciousness of our God. Because he has lovingly blessed them in the past, does it give them a right to go on resisting his will to reunite his Church? Let them come back to the Mother Church, bringing their blessings and insights with them so as to enrich us all in the Lord's work. The protestant schism *must* come to an end; and I believe it will happen as individual protestants respond one-by-one to the call of God.

Traditional barriers

The protestant Churches include within their ranks a wide variety of religious approaches; these range from a liberalism that likes to examine critically all the accepted foundations and takes nothing for granted, to an anglo-catholicism with a fully formed sacramental life. The one thing they have in common is *not* wishing to be under the control of Rome. Indeed from the time of the Reformation there have been those in the English Church whose protest is simply against the running of their Church from outside. Henry VIII was the first of these. They have nothing against catholics or any other group of Christians, as long as the English Church is controlled by Englishmen!

Such protestants would not accept any scheme of Church reunion unless Rome conceded a federalism that left the English Church free to do (and believe) what it wished. They just want to be English and independent – all very patriotic, and typically human, but not the way to share in a worldwide mission. The actual effect of such independence is to justify any pattern of belief (or unbelief) as long as it is English. The present chaos of beliefs in the Church of England shows where that sort of protestantism leads. There is little one can say to it, for it refuses to take seriously the imperative of Christ to unite his Church.

The people in the Church of England who are closest to Rome are the anglo-catholics. They value the inherited sacramental pattern of the

Church's worship, and use it faithfully and well. Henry VIII and Elizabeth I both clung tenaciously to the ancient forms, even while they
worked to separate their Church from Rome. There have always been
those in the Church of England who sought to preserve the old religion;
and most of them secretly hoped for eventual reunion. They kept the
door open through centuries when all the pressure of nationalistic
protestantism was trying to slam it shut for ever. They have won some
important battles. For instance the Holy Communion is now fairly generally restored as the Church of England's main act of worship. Also
they have stood for dignity and quality in worship and in the design of
churches; and they have kept alive for us all wider traditions of prayer
and spirituality.

However, Rome has been changing so rapidly in recent years that
many anglo-catholic clergy have lagged behind and are now rather out
of date. Some of them rather enjoy their fine old-fashioned ways. So
they stay in the Church of England, where a parson can do just what he
likes, and nobody can stop him! If they became Roman Catholics they
would have to conform. I am sure, however, that most of them will do so
eventually.

Anti-Roman prejudice runs deep in the hearts of protestants; and this
is not surprising. For it is barely 250 years since we fought bloody battles over the succession to the throne – when protestants (with a
Hanoverian king) resisted the claims of papists (with a Stuart Pre-
tender). The papists were viewed then as foreigners and traitors, out to
subvert and take over the English State. Fear of popery has now evapo-
rated; but it has left a stain in the minds of protestants that makes it hard
for them to be rational about catholics.

The most commonly voiced doctrinal difficulty for protestants is
papal infallibility. We have talked of this earlier (pages 64–6). But it is
worth repeating that catholics do not claim the ordinary utterances of
Popes as infallible, though they are treated with great respect. That
description is reserved for the rare occasions when the Pope expresses
the mind and faith of the whole Church after lengthy consultation.
Every Church needs a way of settling difficult matters of doctrine. The
Methodists use their Conference; the Church of England, its General
Synod. And catholics look to the Pope to make such decisions, after due
consultation with his bishops. Nobody claims the General Synod as
infallible, though for the Church of England the effect of its decisions is
the same. Papal infallibility is a statement of faith that God will not
allow the Church founded on Peter to go astray.

For most people protestant prejudice focuses on a small number of traditional catholic practices, like the confessional. Here is something that the Church of England too has always kept available, as the Book of Common Prayer makes clear. But evangelicals and nonconformists view the practice with suspicion. However, call it by a another name, counselling, and they have no problem. Catholics partly retain the old formal way of making confessions; but alongside it they tend more and more to adopt a style of talking face to face with the priest across a table. I think protestants would call this counselling! All Christians need from time to time to talk over their spiritual progress with someone else; for most of us it is the only way we will ever overcome our all-too-human blindness. Protestants know this just as well as catholics.

Nonetheless protestants still fear the power over the consciences of the people that they suppose the Roman system gives to the priest – and behind him to the Pope. For instance they are uneasy about the catholic teaching on contraception. The world at large is furious with the Pope for the line he takes in this matter, seeing over-population as the source of many of the world's troubles. But the world is passing through a revolution in which all the old social ethics are in the melting pot. There has probably never been a time when ordinary people were more uncertain about the rights and wrongs of sexual behaviour. Protestants should think twice before siding with the world against a Pope who is doing nothing more than standing fearlessly for traditional Bible-based morality. They would do well first to read what the Pope really has taught (e.g. in his encyclicals *Veritatis Splendor* and *Evangelium Vitae*). They should have a chat with some modern catholics about it, who, like everyone else, have their consciences formed by many influences. The debate continues – inside and outside the Catholic Church – and no infallible proclamation has been made. Few catholics seem to feel the authority of their Church as a threat, in this or in any other matter. They treat the Pope and the priests with great respect, particularly in their teaching roles; but most of them reckon to decide things in their own consciences, and live their lives accordingly. What else should any Christian do?

Some clergy have difficulties over the Roman approach to law. Certainly the Code of Canon Law of the Catholic Church is one of the most daunting documents in the world! And it is particularly daunting for English people, whose concept of law is quite different from that of Mediterranean people – as our politicians who work with European colleagues continually discover to their cost. We like our laws to be a bit vague; and this allows room for the details to be settled by real cases that come before the courts. Most of our Common Law is of this kind, not fixed by Act of Parliament but by cases decided in the courts down the centuries. It is the way we keep our legal system human. The Latin races have a completely different approach: they like their laws to be exact; and they write them with a precision that leaves Anglo-Saxons gasping! But then, real life exists for them in another compartment, and is to be lived by real people in real situations. They too like their legal system to be human, and they know that you cannot ultimately control life by law; and in this they are embracing a principle that is by no means alien to the Gospel of Christ. The rules of the Church of England are flexible and full of room for exceptions. The Roman Canons are rigid, but are applied by human beings. For instance, marriage for catholics is indissoluble, and divorce impossible. But in actual marriage breakdowns, the situation is often handled much more humanely and pastorally than in the Church of England. For Anglicans the Canon Law is a strange and alien world of thought; but they soon find that it is in fact operated by human beings who know as much about the love of Christ as anyone.

There are probably no two people in the Church of England, or in the protestant world generally, who share quite the same problem in considering the path back to Rome. Many sense a disintegration going on in English Church life, and are drawn to the strength and stability of the universal Church. They see many of the traditional barriers between protestants and catholics as historical relics they can now safely ignore; and they feel strongly the call to return to the historic fold of the Catholic Church. But they have some serious remaining difficulties. Probably there always will be difficulties; perhaps the Lord will make sure of it! For I believe he wants us to feel the imperative to return to the universal Church as more important than anything else. Only when we make the move do the final difficulties evaporate.

People face all sorts of practical problems as they come to such a decision. They have obligations to their fellow-Christians in various ways. They have families to consider, and friends who will find it hard to understand. Some have roles in the local church – as treasurers, church-wardens, etc. – and feel they cannot suddenly shed their responsibilities. Some need time to weigh up carefully what the Lord is calling them to do. Some lack the mental flexibility for a major change, coming perhaps late in life. So I think it unlikely that the Lord will allow the protestant Churches to collapse suddenly; for it would hurt too many of his flock, whose only intention is to follow humbly in the way of Christ as they understand it. His pressure upon us to come together in the universal Church is very great; but I am sure he means to protect those who lack the resources for a sudden change. Change we must, however, eventually. The Lord insists on unity in his Church, just as once he insisted on reformation. In his own time he will bring it to pass, however much we struggle to put off the day. We are taught to pray that his kingdom will come. So it will!

The cutting edge of the Church

At the centre of protestantism there has always been a clearly thought-out *evangelical* position. These protestants base their discipleship on following our Lord Jesus Christ as revealed in the Bible, and in the Bible only. This was the position worked out by Luther, Calvin and the other Reformers, who were not in the first instance wanting to break up the unity of Christendom. Evangelicals are not necessarily against the Catholic Church – only where they suspect Roman doctrine or practice of being unscriptural. These are the *real* protestants. They have a tendency not to agree among themselves, for the interpreting of Scripture is a difficult task, and each group does it rather differently. These are the protestants to whom I have mostly addressed this book; for I know they can be persuaded by good arguments based on Scripture. It is time for them to look again at the old issues. For they are not really anti-Roman like other protestants: they are simply *for* the Bible, and that puts them *alongside* the catholics, who equally place a high value on the Bible. These evangelical protestants are the ones for whom I particularly have a message.

Likewise I have been writing for catholics who are alert to the new insights opened up by the Second Vatican Council. Respect for Scripture and Tradition is basic to catholicism, and these catholics will be open to anything the Holy Spirit may have to say through the witness of protestants. There are many lay catholics who have not yet caught up with these insights. It may need generations of quiet pastoring before the whole Church comes to see some things as a genuine part of the old tradition. But already there are many who are thrilled by the vision opening up before them.

Much of the history of the last few centuries has been about the two diverging Christian religions, the catholic and the protestant. But now at length our Lord Jesus Christ, who is at work within both traditions, is enabling them to see the truth each stands for. The Christian bond that stands out at the present time is that between the *Evangelical Protestant* and the *Roman Catholic*. Such a statement may raise both evangelical and catholic eyebrows. But we have so much in common together now. We both believe in a God who intervenes in our affairs, supremely in the person of his Son at the Incarnation. We both see the death and resurrection of Christ as the only ground of our forgiveness and hope, and we preach the same Gospel of a Christ who saves. We both see him as the God of history, but also as a personal God, approachable by each one of us. We believe in prayer, and we know we have a God who faithfully responds when we call on him in the name of our Lord Jesus Christ. We both treat the Scriptures as the word of God, an indispensable part of God's direction of his Church. Fellow-evangelicals, you don't realize how Rome has changed! In many ways they are now more evangelical than you are. Fellow-catholics, you don't understand who are your real allies in the wider Church. It is time evangelicals and catholics got together. For here is the true cutting edge of the Church.

The path of obedience
For evangelicals and catholics alike the authority of Scripture is not in dispute. But there are important issues evangelicals have to sort out before they can go further. One question they have to settle is whether revelation really did end with the New Testament. They adopted that position at the Reformation for clear historical reasons; but are they right to stick to it now? I do not think they can produce any *scriptural* argument to support it – indeed quite the reverse. If the Holy Spirit is still active in the Church, then he is still leading the Church into all truth. The truth about our God was never going to be confined by the mental resources and culture of any one generation. Doctrine must conform to the Bible, but will never be limited by it.

Another question evangelicals have to ask is: 'What form of Church structure and government was our Lord Jesus Christ pointing to in the Gospels?' The Petrine text of Matthew 16 is by no means the only one that suggests the kind of structure we see in the Catholic Church. Given that the Holy Spirit still had to lead the Church into his chosen historical situation, what we see is not inconsistent with the teaching of the Bible. Should we ask for more? The Roman Church rejoices to be founded jointly on the Apostles Peter and Paul: Peter the Apostle to the Jews, Paul to the Gentiles (Gal 2:7–9). There was endless tension between Jewish and Gentile Christians throughout the New Testament period. Finally at Rome the two strands of Christianity were brought together by their Apostles. If you stop to think about it, St Luke makes much of this in the way he selects his material for the Acts of the Apostles. The authority to unite the Church does indeed rest in the Church of Rome in a quite special historical way.

The conclusion of the matter

In the last analysis the decision we make is a matter of loyalty and faithfulness – those personal qualities that underwrite all true relationships. We must be loyal to our Lord Jesus Christ and faithful to the revelation of God he has brought us. There is no other signpost any Christian dare follow. We follow it knowing that he has proved himself loyal and faithful to us beyond anything that could be imagined.

We live in a time of revolution, both in society and in the Church. It is a time when Christians are easily rushed into quick solutions. But there is no quick answer; for the Lord is creating his own new pattern according to his timetable, not ours. If we are to be part of it, the only way is a quiet, prayerful, step-by-step obedience, neither hurrying ahead of him nor lagging behind. As so often in times of spiritual upheaval there are no clear guidelines to quote – only the obligation to follow loyally the light we have. The Lord is able to assess whether we are being obedient or are just following our own inclinations. His assessment is the only test that matters; and we may not judge one another. It is usually a lonely decision, and we are not to look over our shoulders at the way others are going; the future is unlikely to be with majorities – more usually the Lord works through the few. The only safety is in a close walk with him.

St Paul, that most ardent and balanced of pioneers, had it right – and notice, he allowed plenty of room for those who thought differently:

> I press on to take hold of that for which Christ Jesus took hold of me. . . . one thing I do: Forgetting what is behind and straining towards what is ahead, I press on towards the goal to win the prize for which God has called me heavenwards in Christ Jesus. All of us who are mature should take such a view of things. And if on some point you think differently, that too God will make clear to you. (Phil 3:12–15)

I believe our loving God is offering us a unique opportunity to set right the Church failures of the last few centuries. Christians in England share a rather special mixture of respect for tradition and flexibility of outlook; we are still the *frontier Church*, out here *on the fringe*. We need an adventurous approach if we are to take the opportunity the Lord is giving us, and point the way for others. A radical coming home of English Christians into the universal Church would indeed alter the whole outlook of world Christianity. For many people the very idea still seems like cultural suicide. But, as St Cuthbert showed, nothing good and true can possibly be lost in such a process. If we are to embrace the future *for which Christ Jesus took hold of us* more than thirteen centuries ago, we must find the resources in the Church that will save our people from the secular morass into which they are sinking, and so perhaps discover a new righteousness to face a world in crisis.

SCRIPTURE AND CATECHISM REFERENCES

INDEX